MARIA CRISTINA ALFIERI ROSSELLA CATTANI
MILENA FORNARI

PARMA

History, art and monuments

by

LUCIA FORNARI SCHIANCHI

Published by
ITALCARDS
bologna Italy

The aerial photograph clearly outlines the present urban layout of the city. In the centre is the Parma river which divides it vertically, at the bottom right-hand corner the wide green lung of the Duke's Park, at the top left-hand corner the pentagonal shape of the citadel. The urban layout still clearly shows the characters of Roman town-planning: the cardo, the present via Farini-Cavour and the decumanus, the via Emilia, which in this part is called via della Repubblica-Mazzini-D'Azeglio, and represents the axis which crosses horizontally the whole city, with the intersection point identifiable in the Piazza Garibaldi.

Ripresa aerofotogrammaetrica della Compagnia Generale Ripreseaeree
Parma - conc. S.M.A. n. 68 del 20.02.78.

FOREWORD

Parma is as fine as every town in the Po Valley, Veneto, Umbria, it's as fine as every part of Italy. Italy is the centre of a millenary civilization, whose traits you can still find everywhere in the town planning and in the temper of its inhabitants.

Constantly Parma remembers its myths: heroicness, elegance, music, cooking and... if once the tourist doesn't meet one of these looks he may be disappointed; he may be deprived of an image that is stronger than the same contemporaneity, whose signs you can see in a particular way of life you can rarely find. This way of life is typical in Parma, it means spontaneity, eros, revolutionary courage, good sense, joy and historical awareness, hard-working knowledge and real taste of life.

Here's another myth for this town that charmed Stendhal and Proust, it can't live far from the mystery and needs to look at itself in the mirror every day, it needs to tell about itself: it's a vain and pedantic town but surely generous and joyful, it's sometimes mild, often aggressive.

If you arrive by plane, as it often happens nowadays, the view of the old town looks homogeneous, with something new, breaking the warm atmosphere of the long rows of roofs and bell towers, its roof terraces and pink marble spires all surrounded by narrow outskirts, here and there you can see big green areas and the river that seems widening and enlighting the town, the bridges in the direction of the Apennines southwards and the Pre-Alps northwards.

This river, which is sometimes full of slimy water and sometimes dry in its stony bottom, sometimes clean, is the symbol of the two parts of the town, the noble and oldest with Palazzo della Pilotta, a very strict building with a lot of courts inside, and the most popular one growing along the Parma near the Church of Annunciata, Santa Maria del Quartiere, Ospedale Vecchio and Santa Maria delle Grazie.

In the old part of the town you can see Verona marble and sandstone worked by skilled artisans, who build houses with bricks and lay down its wide cobblestone pavements, sometimes cut from compact stone riding rails, that are greyish and unassailable. The plasters are added little by little, mostly painted yellow, as they used in France and in Austria, and then the neoclassic fronts, the walking places, the rows of planes and poplars, of elms and limes, of maples, of horse-chestnuts, which a few rare cedar of Lebanon are added to, together with some Ginkgo biloba and some monumental magnolia: the natural architecture and the built one are defined; Parma remains an ancient town and becomes an up-to-date town at the same time, by building up some service, transport and big industrial centres in its outskirts.

4

equipping itself with buildings without solemnity, but functional for the life of the economical exchanges and of the productivity that are competing in Europe and in the whole world.

Parma still follows its historical vocation, it exploits its geographical vocation refusing the role of provinciality firmly. It refuses this role connecting with the big centres in the Northern part of Italy, it's always full of development projects but it never refuses the strongest project.

This last project, that is the harmony between the past and the present, is inherent in the people of Parma. The mirror was the symbol of its most important painter, Parmigianino, and now the mirror must reflect the harmonious figure of heroine and mother. In 1500 in his allegory of the town, Bedoli describes Parma like Minerva-Venus welcoming its inhabitants and tourists who want to remain here, but it lets them go if they want to go away feeling oppressed here.

A town is always difficult to define, because it is made of men, powers, balances that change, even if slowly, and then it becomes easier to stop the atmospheres that vary from season to season: summertime, hot, in the late afternoon in the cafeterias in Garibaldi Square, or under the planes of Parco Ducale, or in some swimming pool clubs; wintertime at Teatro Regio or in the renewed halls of the Galleria Nazionale; springtime going by bike along the avenues; autumntime in the Cittadella, where the sun sets down late: it is a town made of half tones, of lights and shades of outlines blurring fogs, that make the reality less bright and hard, a bit vague, unreal: a reality where you can still smile, as certain heroes of Verdi who do not belong to the myth of melodramma, but they come on the scene as human strength. A humanity that smiles at us in this aware and responsible town: the town is not the rippled outline we see arriving by plane, but it is the reality of its suburbs, its squares, its citizens aside from the age and the profession, from the classes and the social condition. The true town is the one which moves, talks, decides among great monuments, that nobody has ever dared to scratch or to transform, over the centuries, giving us, in this way, the true sense of history.

In this guide we tell the town to its visitors; we recommend them to meet it outside and inside its myths, so that the town can appear in all its possible aspects and the desire of discovery and of personal way of describing, that is in all of us, can be satisfied.

The town is under our eyes, let's look at it plainly.

LUCIA FORNARI SCHIANCHI

History of Parma

ANCIENT PARMA

Parma lies in Italy's western Emilia where traces of the Paleolithic have been discovered in the Apennines foot-hills. Present data reveal nothing of the Early Neolithic, while the Middle and Late Neolithic are represented by square-lipped vessels. Very few artifacts of the Early Bronze Age have come to light, although the Middle and Late Bronze Age artifacts bear witness to the Terramare culture (from *terra marna*, the dark soil of these settlements used as fertilizer until the last century). These traces comprise evidence of wooden pile dwellings, as Parma was an important road junction at the foot of the mountains. Still obscure is the link between the Late Bronze Age and the Early Villanova culture that was discovered near Bologna. In the Late Iron Age (4th cent. BC), the Celts began settling the area and upsetting the equilibrium among the previously established centres of population.

After the defeat of the Gauls in the 2nd cent. BC, the Romans surveyed the land *(centuriatio)*, divided it into plots or *jugera* (1 *jugerum = ca.* 2500 m²) and founded the colony of Parma in 183 BC. Thus, the Romans completed the occupation on both sides of the Via Emilia roadway, that stretched from Rimini to Piacenza by 187 BC. The Roman survey followed the road and included the areas lying along the Enza, Taro and Po rivers and up to the Apennines, encouraging land reclamation as a result. The four compass points of this division can still be seen today in Parma, as in other cities of the Emilia. Via Farini - Via Cavour is the north-south and Via Repubblica - Via Mazzini - Via Massimo D'Azeglio the east-west axis. Their intersection, which coincided with the city's Roman forum, is partially discernible as Piazza Garibaldi.

The Roman colony reached its apex under the Emperor Augustus. He fostered its economic development by founding the Veleia free-trade outpost and providing the city with a stone bridge spanning its river. The remains of the bridge are visible in today's Via Mazzini underpass. The only other clearly identified traces of public works are those belonging to the theatre near the church of San Uldarico and those of the amphitheatre on the site now occupied by the Collegio Maria Luigia.

The city's decline starts in the 2nd cent. AD, coinciding with a general economic crisis of the Empire. Subsequently, under the brief Byzantine interregnum (553-568), Parma is renamed Chrisopolis, or golden city, perhaps a reference to its being the seat of the military tax service. This period also saw changes in the once lush countryside. The unchecked advance of marshes and forests had disastrous consequences on the local economy and brought about a clear-cut division between the declining city and outlying country. The Langobards succeeded the Byzantines in 570 and settled in the north-east area of the city near the river, probably at the end of today's Via Repubblica. The church of San Michele, a popular Langobard saint, would seem to bear this out.

1

1. The prototype of the town bricks bricked up in the Palazzo del Governatore formerly dei Mercanti. 2. Via Cardinal Ferrari: on the right the southern side of Duomo; in the background Battistero and Palazzo Vescovile.

MEDIEVAL PARMA

Under the Carolingians Parma was governed by the count-bishop. In 879 Carloman grants Bishop Guibodo temporal power over the city, later extending it to the outlying territories or *suburbia*. After the 1037 uprising against the town's episcopal government, Bishop Cadalo (1048-1077), elected the Anti-Pope as Honorius II, transferred his residence to a defensive position north of the city walls in the *Pratum regium*, the former Langobard site of markets, jousts and tournaments. The new episcopal seat, restored several times over the centuries, was a virtual castle. Rectangular in plan, it featured fortifications, towers, moat and, inside, a xenodochium or guest-house, chapel and prison. The surviving records of the present-day Cathedral, which was erected in front of the castle, date to 1092, although it is definitely older. Next to it stood the *canonicale claustrum* or common residence of the clergy.

The city walls were enlarged in 1169 to incorporate the new suburbs, their monasteries of **San Giovanni** (980), **San Paolo** (985) and **San Sepolcro** and the *Platea Ecclesia Maioris* or **Piazza Duomo**. This square took on its present-day aspect with the closing of the south end by the erection of the **Battistero** or Baptistery (c. 1196-1270). At the time of its completion, however, the Piazza Duomo or square was the town's virtual centre, uniting the temporal and religious powers in the person of the count-bishop and being able to accommodate the entire citizenry within it. At the south-eastern edge of the town, once occupied by the Arena or amphitheatre, Emperor Frederick I Barbarossa ordered the construction of a fortified palazzo (1158-1162), symbol of imperial power. This area, however, also marks the rise of the Communes or city-states, and Parma is no exception. The Commune takes possession of the ancient forum long in disuse and thereupon erects the first municipal buildings. The old Roman centre had been revived and, with it, the purely secular spirit of a new age took form. The first **Palazzo Comunale** or town hall, seat of the Consiglio di Credenza or city council, was situated on the corner of the present-day Via Repubblica and Via Cavour.

The **Piazza del Comune** or town square took on its present-day dimensions between 1221 and 1285 with the completion of the **Palazzo del Torello** (named for Torello da Strada, the first podestà or chief magistrate) on the south-west corner. Its portico, opposite the church of San Pietro whose apse faced the piazza, was used as a halting-place for soldiers and «brentatori», men who carried casks of wine or fire water. Thereafter, the **Palazzo del Podestà**, with its communicating gallery to **Palazzo del Torello**, the tower (which collapsed in 1606), and the **Palazzo del Capitano del Popolo**, destroyed by the tower's collapse, went up on the south side, and the **Palazzo dei Mercanti**, later **Palazzo del Governatore**, on the north. The façade bricks of the Merchant Guild Hall are of a standard size and were originally used as measures. To finance these works, the City Council decreed that anyone wishing to become a citizen of Parma had to deposit a tenth of their worldly goods.

The devastating flood of 1177 narrowed the river's bed near the Roman bridge, thereby changing the face of the town's plan. It created, that is, a new public area that was called the «Glara», meaning the gravel of its natural paving. This square was first used as the site of public executions — the famous burning at the stake of two women heretics and the ensuing riots among them. From about 1308, the square is used mostly as a livestock market, a function it will retain up to the 19th century. The rest of the river-bed area soon underwent a building boom. Construction works sprawled outward from it in a fan and, in 1210, were incorporated within the newly ex-

---

1. One of the fascinating artistic performances which take place in summer evenings in Piazza Duomo.

panded town walls. This date marks the beginning of the city's development on the **Oltretorrente** side of the river, the «cross-river» area.

Another factor that strongly influenced Parma's medieval plan was the complex system of canals connecting it with the main waterway of the Po river. This system also affected the artisans and craftsmen in their choosing sites for their works.

For example, the wool workers set up shop at the edge of town by the Naviglio, where the two main canals converged carrying off the effluents from the dye-works. Even their dwellings felt the effects. Called Gothic-style row houses, they were tall, narrow single-family units whose side walls were shared by the abutting houses. They featured a street entrance, shop and, in the back, a garden that gave on to either a canal or a road. The façade often had an arcade that was used as both the shop's sales-counter and covered walk-way.

The progressive extension of these suburban artisan districts made it necessary to enlarge the town's walls first in 1230 and again in 1261, where they remained unchanged till the early 20th century.

1. Piazza Duomo with Palazzo Vescovile on the left-hand and Battistero on the background. 2. B.go delle Colonne. One of the streets of the gothic part. 3. B.go del Naviglio. 4. Ghiaia weekly market.

3

PARMA AND THE SIGNORIA

The waning of the *Commune* in the late 13th and early decades of the 14th centuries led to the subsequent rise of the *Signoria*, rule by a single patrician family or lord. This process was a gradual one and began with the strengthening of the traditionally powerful rural aristocracy whose influence was constant and, to a large extent, decisive in the events shaping local history at least up to the age of the Farnese family. In the surrounding countryside, the noble Rossi, Sanvitale, da Correggio and Pallavicino families had long established territorial dominion by rule of a lord or *Signoria* — a system that had always been independent of the city's government and its institutions but not of the struggle for power over them. With the changing of the guard from *Commune* to *Signoria*, Parma found itself at the mercy of factional imperatives that carved up its territory politically and precluded its becoming an independent principality historically — not to mention de-

4

fending itself from outside intervention militarily. Thus it was that the town was annexed to the Duchy of Milan and kept under Visconti rule from 1346 to 1447 and under the Sforzas from 1449 to 1499.

The new government's policy of centralisation was immediately directed towards refeudalisation and the consequent incorporation of the rural *Signoria* systems through a reinstating of the old vassal bonds. The local aristocracy, however, proved recalcitrant, unwilling to don the feudal yoke of submission. The historical records of the period reveal a predominant defensive attitude by the government — a posture that stemmed as much from Parma's strategic position as a border area within the duchy as from the aristocracy's citadels that rose threateningly not far from the city walls. These were reinforced over and over again by Luchino Visconti, who even strengthened the piazza or square until it became a veritable fortress called **Keep-the-peace**, later demolished under the Farnese. Fortresses were also built at Santa Croce, Porta San Michele and Porta Nuova, while fortified positions were erected in the northwest part of the city.

These latter were first planned in all likelihood by Bernabò Visconti, but actually brought to completion by Galeazzo Maria Sforza. They included the castle, a site now occupied by the **Palazzo del Giardino**, and the two *racchette* or small forts situated at the west (still visible) and larger one at the east (now part of the Palazzo della Pilotta) ends of the Galleria (now Verdi) bridge.

Meanwhile, the *Signorias* in the surrounding countryside were finding their castles to

be the most effective instruments in power politics. Those of the Rossi family at **Torrechiara, Roccabianca, San Secondo** and that of the Terzis at **Montechiarugolo** date to this period. Very different in style from the rough fortresses of the previous ages, they were manors, stylish and exclusive courts destined to become the collective home of Humanism at Parma during the 14-1500s. The political and cultural role of the *Signorias* grows stronger in the first decades of the XVI cen-

1. Air view of the historical centre with the medieval tower of Palazzo Vescovile, Duomo and Battistero. 2. The Rocchetta. 2

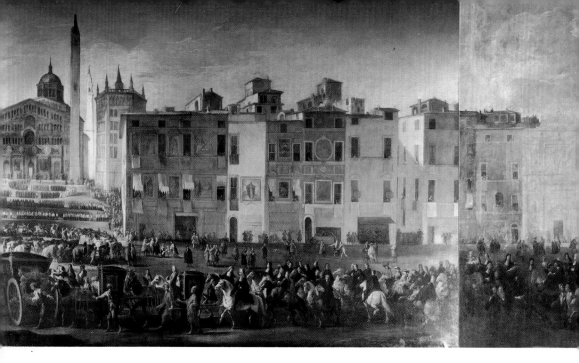

tury — a period that was one of the most diffi-cult in Parma's history, marked as it was by the absence or at best by the utter instability of a central power.

From 1499 to the beginning of Farnese rule in 1545, Parma was caught in the power struggle between France, victor over the Duchy of Milan, and the Papacy, ally of Spain. The city and its surrounding territory even became a theatre of battle in the repeated armed conflicts of both sides, which took turns in governing the area. The local aristoc-racy once again exploited the political inst-ability to its advantage by putting pressure on local government through the influence of the city's numerous Benedictine institutions. Their total number was five: four were con-vents for women only and one, San Giovanni, a monastery for men. In the hands of the aris-tocracy's younger sons, the «cloisters and cas-tles» became important and often opposing centres of political power and cultural deve-lopment. Correggio's works in San Paolo and San Giovanni are but one example.

THE FARNESE FAMILY

The Duchy of Parma and Piacenza was conceived by temporal and spiritual design in the 1543 meeting at Busseto between the Em-peror Charles V and Pope Paul III, Alessan-dro Farnese, and brought into being in 1545 when the Pope's son, Pier Luigi, claimed his duchy for services rendered as *gonfalonier* or standard-bearing knight of the Church. Rath-er than pride, the new arrival aroused only hostility — of the neighbouring Este and Gon-zaga families, of the imperial power itself and, chiefly, of the local nobility.

As internal dissension raised its head, the new duke raised his sword to sever it. He de-prived the feudal nobles of their right to ad-minister justice, forced them to take up resid-ence in the city, levied heavy taxes upon them and created a new loyalist aristocracy to sup-plant them. He further sought to strengthen his hand, if not his head, by razing within a half-mile radius the precincts, dwellings and religious houses that had sprung up hapha-zardly about the city's walls, thus making it ea-sier to defend the town and encouraging fu-ture development.

1. Photographic assembly of three paintings of court «chronic-ler» I. Spolverini. You can see here the procession running along the present Via Repubblica and Via Cavour for the wedding of Elisabetta Farnese with Philip V of Spain. (1714)

While the duke planned his policies with determination, the local nobility plotted his demise with vengeance. Pier Luigi was assassinated at Piacenza in 1547. His death marked a turning point for both the city and the duchy. Until then, the court had divided its residence between Parma and Piacenza. Thereafter, the permanent seat of government would be Parma.

Ottavio Farnese (1547-1586), who succeeded Pier Luigi, established temporary residence in a group of expropriated houses near the Rocchetta or stronghold — the present-day area between Via Cavour and the Palazzo della Pilotta. While the question of where and when the permanent royal palazzo was to be built was postponed indefinitely, Ottavio showed no such hesitation in ordering the erection of a temporary court. Designed by the architect Vignola, it was begun in 1561 at Co' di Ponte, a wooded, undeveloped site once occupied by the Sforza Castle. Ottavio, and the other Farnese dukes after him, continued to develop the so-called «Oltretorrente» or «cross-river» land. Traditionally left to the course of nature and the ramshackle dwellings of the poor, the zone was transformed by Farnese policy. Important structures such as the churches of **Santissima Annunziata** (Annunciation) and **Santa**

Maria del Quartiere were built there in 1566 and 1604, respectively, and, in 1580, Ottavio ordered the construction of a «corridor» — vaguely resembling the plan of the Medici court complex — linking the two palazzi.

Ottavio was succeeded by Alessandro (1586-92). As Philip II's general and governor of the Low Countries, he was largely absent from his duchy. This explains why he never completed the «palazzo ducale» but, as an expert in fortifications, did endow the city with, and probably design, a pentagonal fort called the «**Cittadella**» (1591). About three thousand people were employed in its building and paid directly from the duke's personal coffers — an attempt to remedy the harsh living conditions and intolerable rate of unemployment brought about by relentless wars, famines and epidemics.

Alessandro's son Ranuccio (1592-1622) completed the Farnese residences with the construction of a vast building called **Palazzo della Pilotta**. Planned as a «general service» complex, this massive structure has become the symbol of ducal «absolutism» for the way in which, then as now, it violates the city's plan. Thereafter, Ranuccio completed the city's defences that began with the «Cittadella» fort by having his architect, G. Bresciani, design — to the most advanced concepts of the day's military architecture — and build four towering bulwarks along the north-eastern walls. The core of the old city centre was finally ringed by impregnable fortifications, and the walls themselves would stand virtually unaltered from then until the early 20th century.

In 1612, Ranuccio's autocratic centralisation of power led to a bloody repression of the local nobility in the wake of an alleged plot against the duke. As the death sentence was passed against Barbara Sanseverino, one of the aristocracy's most prominent exponents, her family's estate at Colorno passed into the hands of the duke. After extensive alterations and remodelling, the original fortress was transformed into the duke's amenable summer residence.

As patrons of the arts, the first Farnese dukes left their mark on the city in other ways, too. Their patronage included the vast 16th-century palazzi that altered forever the medieval character of the old city, and the introduction of a stimulating cultural environment through the bringing to Parma of predominantly Roman artists who had worked on the Farnese palazzi at Rome and Caprarola. The political isolation and economic depression that followed the death of Ranuccio marked the beginning of an inexorable decline that his successors proved powerless to check.

The golden age was over. Parma and its last Farnese dukes spent their days in pursuit of ephemeral splendour — feasts, spectacles and pageantry set against the backdrop of the city became the major affairs of state at a decadent court. The last descendant of the family, Antonio (1727-31), left no sons upon his death, and the duchy was inherited by Charles of Bourbon, son of Elisabetta Farnese and Philip V, in accordance with the 1720 Treaty of the Hague. In 1732 he arrived in triumph to take possession of his duchy; in 1734 he left in haste to claim his kingdom. But he did not go empty-handed. The Bourbon court at Naples (the Kingdom of Naples and Sicily) boasted the art collections and furnishings that the new king had literally stripped from the royal estates of Parma, Piacenza, Colorno and Sala.

THE BOURBONS

After the peace of Aix-la-Chapelle in 1748 and the brief interregnum that followed, the duchy, which then included the newly-annexed town of Guastalla, was returned to Bourbon control under Philip (1749-1765) the younger son of Elisabetta Farnese. He is soon joined at Parma by his wife Louise Elisabeth, daughter of the French king Louis XV. French tastes and style will become the order of the day, as the new duchess summons numerous artists and craftsmen from Paris to replace and revive what Charles had left empty and bare.

The same remedy was also applied to the dire state of the duchy's economic and social conditions. Appointed prime minister in 1759, Guillaume Du Tillot brought the Enlightenment and its principles to bear on resuscitating the finances — exhausted by the megalomania of the Farneses — and promoting industry and agriculture.

Nor was the cultural domain left out of the grand design. He envisioned a Parma that would play, via close links to Paris, a role on the European level. To this end he founded a number of secular institutions: the **Accademia delle Belle Arti** (1752) or Academy of Fine Arts, which attracted artists of international renown, including Goya, to its competitions; the **Collegio Lalatta** (1755); the **Biblioteca Palatina** (1762) or Palatine Library; the Museo di Antichità (1763) or Museum of Antiquities, established to house the archaeological discoveries at Veleia; the **Stamperia Ducale** (1768) or Court Printing Press, set up in recognition of Bodoni; and the **Orto Botanico** (1768) or Botanical Gardens. Many of these institutions were, and still are, housed in the Palazzo della Pilotta.

Du Tillot did not stop there in pursuit of his goals. He had the Jesuits, who had had a virtual monopoly on education in the city, banned from Parma and their estates confiscated. What had been their College of San Rocco now became the seat of the University.

Even town planning came under the far-reaching influence of Du Tillot's policies. What had been haphazard urban sprawl and

1 decay up to Bourbon rule, was thenceforth slated for renewal. Though the policy was the prime minister's, the architect who implemented it was Ennemond Alexandre Petitot, summoned to the court from France in 1753. Under his direction, Parma soon took on the new features of the emerging neoclassical style. After restoring the royal palazzi at Parma and Colorno, and designing the **Casino dei Boschi at Sala**, he set about revamping strategic points within Parma. In Piazza Garibaldi (formerly Piazza Grande), he redesigned the façades of the palazzi, transformed the church of San Pietro whose apse then gave on to it, and placed the *Ara dell'Amicizia* or *Friendship Memorial Altar* (replaced at the height of republican fervour in 1893 by the monument to Garibaldi). His, too, is the tree-lined avenue-cum-promenade (the present-day Stradone) that leads to the **Casino**, a country setting that's ideal for a pause and conversation. He even planned a magnificent royal palace, though it was never built.

Some elements of these policies and practises were later adopted by the Builders' Committee, which was founded in 1767 to oversee private construction. It sought to regulate building height and impose uniform plastering of outside facing, so as to give the city a modern aspect.

The marriage of Ferdinand of Bourbon (1765-1802), Philip's son, and Maria Amalia, daughter of Maria Theresa of Austria, marked the end of French and the beginning of Austrian influence. Du Tillot and the Enlightenment were put out, and a policy of «restoration» was installed: the return of the economy to a standstill and of the banned religious orders to the city.

When Napoleon entered Parma in 1796, he acknowledged Ferdinand's neutrality by letting him rule until his death six years later. Moreau de Saint Mèry, «administrator general» of the duchy, cautiously introduces insti-

tutional changes designed to revive the territory's lagging resources. He first imposes heavy taxes and promotes traditional industries. Then, by a 1810 imperial decree, he bans certain religious orders, confiscates their property and secularizes the works of charity by uniting them in the Administration of Civil Hospices.

A concrete example of this aspect can be seen in the transformation of the monastery of San Francesco del Prato into a prison.

MARIE LOUISE

The Congress of Vienna (1815) awarded the Duchy of Parma to Marie Louise, daughter of the Emperor of Austria Francis I and Napoleon's wife, although it was stipulated that at her death the kingdom be returned to the Bourbons of Lucca. Beloved by her subjects, and even today celebrated as a legendary figure, she championed a policy of benign public welfare. This was true also of her public works projects which, while designed

Galleria Nazionale G.B. Borghesi. Portrait of Maria Luigia Duchess of Parma. 1

to bring order and beautify the city's landscape, aimed as well to alleviate glaring social ills by creating new jobs.

Perhaps her most significant public works initiative was the 1837 **«Beccherie»** or slaughterhouse project in Piazza Ghiaia. Designed by N. Bettoli, it was the first functionally modern complex of this type, as it housed in a single structure all the city's slaughterhouses. It also caused the livestock market in Piazza Ghiaia to be transferred to Foro Boario (1838), which she had erected on her own land situated between the Ducal Gardens and the river-bed. Her other public works of interest are the **Cimitero della Villetta** (cemetery) designed by G. Cocconcelli in 1817; the **Bridge over the Taro** river, designed by A. Cocconcelli; in the Palazzo della Pilotta, the **Galleria dell'Accademia di Belle Arti** or Gallery of the Academy of Fine Arts (the present-day Galleria Nazionale or National Gallery), the **Biblioteca Ducale** or Ducal Library (today's Sala Maria Luigia or the Marie Louise Wing of the Palatine Library), and the restoration of the Museum of Antiquities; the **Collegio Maria Luigia** (1831); the erection of the famous **Teatro Regio** (1821-28) or Royal Theatre, designed by N. Bettoli; and the Bettoli-designed façade of the Ducal Palace, thus completing a project begun almost three centuries before. The palazzo was destroyed in World War II — the bombing even left a big crack in the Piazzale or large square in front of the Pilotta.

She also promoted uniform face-work on the townhouses of the upper classes along the city's main thoroughfares (the lower classes followed medieval tradition by continuing to live in the Gothic district and the precincts beyond the river). Her court architects — especially N. Bettoli and P. Gazzola — completed the neoclassical revamping begun by Petitot, while underscoring the stylistic unity of the works dating to the period.

THE RETURN OF THE BOURBONS

After the brief rule of Charles II, who succeeded Marie Louise upon her death in 1847, Charles III became king and literally turned the city into an armed camp. He transforme the monasteries of Sts Paolo and Rocco int barracks and used part of the Palazzo della P lotta to billet troops. The hostility aroused b this policy was such that it culminated in hi assassination in 1854.

Louise Marie de Berry, his wife, ruled th duchy as regent for her son. She completel reversed her husband's policy by establishin a prudent neutrality, and fostering the con struction of public works to ease the hars poverty and squalid housing of the lowe classes. Her name is associated with the layin of a new road in the area beyond the river, th **Via della Salute** (1856-1862). Its house were planned and erected to newly-forme progressivist building codes designed to safe guard health standards. Louise Marie in tended the new works to serve as a model fo future development of proletarian housin estates. These plans were interrupted whe the duchess was forced into exile by the an nexation of Parma to Victor Emmanuel II' Kindgom of Savoy.

MODERN PARMA

The present-day aspect of Parma is the re sult of various stages that have taken plac since the unification of Italy and are commo to many other of the country's cities. Apar from such glaring exceptions as the demoli tion of the walls, Parma's urban developmen was undramatic and regular.

At the time of Italy's statehood in 1861 Parma was a pre-industrial city with modes artisan-scale industries still located along th old canals that served both as a power sourc and sewage system. The city's layout is sti substantially medieval in character — tw areas divided by the river. They are both sur rounded by walls and well differentiated so cially and functionally.

With the exception of the **railway's** con struction in 1859, Parma's urban grid re mained almost unchanged for the first thirt years thereafter. However, from 1889 righ up to World War I in 1914, the city underwen a marked real-estate development that radi cally changed its face. The dominant politica

gure during these boom years was mayor
Mariotti, who presided over Parma's «new
look» programmes that would alter the urban
plan with a rapidity wholly unknown to the
gradual changes of the preceding centuries.
The first and most far-reaching was the demo-
tion of the walls in the name of modern progress. This single act alone completely
changed the city's historical layout and paved
the way for future sprawl. Ring-roads that still
delineate the limits of the old city-centre replaced the walls. Beyond them developed ha-
hazardly the industrial buildings near the
railway, the new fashionable residential districts to the south (beyond the Casino Petitot),
and the lower-class housing blocks along the
roads that lead north and east out of Parma.

In this period, the Galleria (now Verdi)
bridge was reconstructed, the new **Bottego**
and **Umberto I** (now Italia) bridges were erected, and the **Lungoparma** was opened by
the road between the Umberto I and Capra-
zucca bridges. These are the early years of the
young Italian nation, a country seeking carve
its identity into the heart of each city by uniting the symbols of progress — the railway,
transport vehicles and urban growth — to its
own new-born myths. It is not by chance that
the erection of the **Verdi Monument**, begun in
1913, is designed to mark the zone that links
the town to the station, an area conceived as
an integral part and continuance of the old
city-centre. This idea of a «vigorous» and
«fashionable» city is behind the «clean-up»
demolitions in the «cross-river» area, not to
mention such public works projects as the
construction of the **hospital** complex in 1915.
It was under Fascism, perhaps, that Parma's
plan underwent one of its most substantial

*The snowy roofs of Palazzo Vescovile, of Duomo and S. Gio-
vanni bell tower.*

changes: the demolition of a large part of the «cross-river» districts that had begun in earlier times. Of strong popular traditions and integrity, these precincts were to become the heart of a stubborn anti-fascism marked by the famous 1922 barricades and the later partisan resistance during World War II for which Parma was awarded the gold medal of valour. In the first two post-war decades, the new socio-political order combined with the damages caused by the war spurred a boom in the city's construction industry, especially in prime real-estate areas. Unfortunately, the period of reconstruction was not used to full advantage by the town planners.

One notable example is Via Mazzini, a street that was built in the early 1960s by demolishing all that stood along the old street called Strada di Bassa dei Magnani. Here, where the via converges on the square, stand two buildings on the west side that are an eyesore with respect to the others about them. It would be extremely difficult to fashion out of these few notes the city's urban development over the last fifty years — a history that would chronicle a town's planning that has not, unlike other Italian cities, developed logically. Rather it has fluctuated between the well-planned growth in the south (Cittadella - Via Solferino) and the unsystematic sprawl of housing and industry into what remains of a well-cared-for countryside in the north.

1. Night view of Piazza Garibaldi with Palazzo del Governatore. 2. View of the covers of Duomo and the Abbazia di San Giovanni on the background.

Piazza Garibaldi

Garibaldi Square and the buildings about it date to the 13th century. Under the Viscontis, fortifications dubbed «sta in pace» or «keep-the-peace» were added. Upon their demolition in 1554, the architect Francesco Testa was commissioned to widen the streets converging on the square. Its original appearance was further altered in 1606 when the tower collapsed, destroying as it fell the city hall palazzo.

PALAZZO COMUNALE

The present town-hall **Palazzo** was designed by Giovan Battista Magnani and owes its construction in 1627-28 to the events surrounding the wedding of Odoardo Farnese and Margherita de' Medici. The first striking thing about it is the exterior brickwork, which it owes to nothing but typical 17th-century Po valley architecture.

It is an imposing rectangle whose mass is move by Doric-like lesenes or pilaster-strips framin arches, panels and niches. The courtyard of th Palazzo Farnese at Piacenza comes to mind as likely inspiration. The ground floor is an open ar cade of piers; and the grand stairway was res tored in 1887. The statue of Correggio (Antoni Allegri) in the niche facing the square is by Agos tino Ferrarini and dates to 1870. The east sid features the statues of **Hercules and Anteu** locked in mythical combat. Popularly called « du brasà» or the embracers, it is a late 16th century work in copper by T. A. Vanderstarch while its arrangement on the tub-like base wa designed by Paolo Toschi during the rule of Ma rie Louise.

The first floor. The Sala del Consiglio or coun cil chamber is decorated with Girolamo Magna ni's and Cecrope Barilli's 19th-century frescos It also features two large paintings by Pier Ilari Spolverini (1657-1734), faithful chronicler o

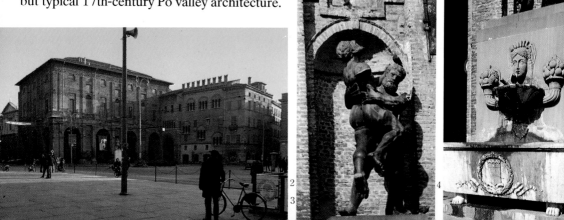

2 3

4

canvas of a decadent court's «last hurrahs». They depict Elisabetta Farnese's wedding procession and nuptials in the Duomo. On display in one of the floor's offices is the Naumachia (mock sea-battle), painted in honour of Odoardo Farnese's royal marriage to Dorothea Sophia of Neuberg. The works portraying the wedding banquet and procession as it approaches Borgotaro can be seen in the atrium, as can be a Crucifixion by Bernardino Gatti and a Nolo me tangere recently attributed to Annibale Carracci, who painted it for the Palazzo Farnese in Rome.

PALAZZO FAINARDI

Originally, this 13th-century building was the **Palazzo del Giudice Criminale** or the medieval criminal court. The populace had dubbed it the «seat of torment», as sentences were carried out in a room called the «curlo» or scream. In the 18th century the court was accommodated elsewhere and the Palazzo was refurbished for private owners.

PALAZZO DEL GOVERNATORE

Seat of the merchants' guild hall and governor's residence when built in the 13th century, it was constructed as two wings separated by an alley called Vicolo San Marco. This was eventually covered by a huge vault in 1606, with the city tower being erected over it in 1673. The palazzo was revamped in 1760 by Ennemond Petitot, who also had it painted in his famous «Parma yellow». The tower's niche holds a terracotta statue of the Madonna and Child (1761) by Jean Baptiste Boudard. It was supposed to have been in marble but proved too expensive. The sundials were added in 1829 to mask some of Petitot's undesired handiwork.

SAN PIETRO APOSTOLO

Dating to the Middle Ages, the Church of St Peter Apostle was given its present façade in 1762 by master-builders Ottavio and Giovanni Bettoli working from the court architect Petitot's design. Neoclassical in style, the front is noteworthy for its four sizeable, pedestaled Corinthian columns, their niche, and the portal crowned by a semicircular dome with coffer-ceiling motif fashioned by the intaglio master Marc Vibert. Above that, the trabeated or post-and-lintel design with dentils and corbels is broken by a large rectangular window and capped by an attic-storey displaying a stucco-work tiara and crossed keys (symbols of St Peter) framed by a laurel-wreath and bay-leaf festoon executed by the court stucco-master Benigno Bossi. Statues of Sts Peter and Paul were to have crowned the façade but were never carried out.

Although the façade never met popular approval at the time, it was, like the alterations to Palazzo del Governatore, part of the court's plan to have Petitot revamp what was then Piazza Grande (Piazza Garibaldi). Here as elsewhere the architect had the building painted yellow — a colour he ably promoted by using it so exclusively that it became along with sky-blue the colour of the city's coat-of-arms.

1. Piazza Garibaldi with the Palazzo del Governatore on the north side, behind it you can see the Steccata dome; on the right a foreshortening of Via Cavour. 2. Piazza Garibaldi. The Town Hall. 3. The Town Hall. The nineteenth-century fountain that is the base of the group of Ercole and Anteo. 4. T.A. Vandersturch; bronze group representing the fight between Hercules and Anteo, it's known among the inhabitants of Parma as «du brasa». 5. Chiesa di San Pietro Apostolo. The front was drawn by E.A. Petitot.

TOUR NO. 1

❶ **Chiesa di S. Lucia** *via Cavour*
❷ **Duomo** *piazza del Duomo*
❸ **Battistero** *piazza del Duomo*
❹ **Palazzo Vescovile** *piazza del Duomo*
❺ **Palazzo del Seminario** *via Cardinal Ferrari*
❻ **Abbazia di S. Giovanni Evangelista** *piazzale S. Giovanni*
❼ **Spezieria di S. Giovanni** *borgo Pipa*
❽ **Chiesa di S. Francesco del Prato** *piazzale S. Francesco*
❾ **Oratorio della Concezione** *via del Prato*

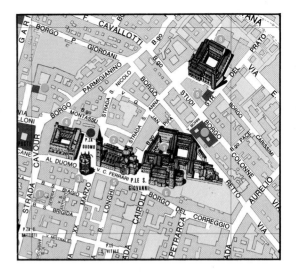

SANTA LUCIA

Although the church was not consecrated until 1697, the façade designed by Mauro Oddi was probably completed by about 1691. The statues of Sts Lucia and Ilario and the high-relief, stucco half-figure of St Agatha in the portal's open-bed pediment are attributed to Giacomo Barbieri, a little-known Baroque sculptor from Lombardy.

The most important work inside is the fine «pala» or high altarpiece depicting the Communion of St Lucy. Painted by Sebastiano Ricci in 1730, it is another example of his subtle and delicate use of colour deliberately recalling the works of Veronese.

THE DUOMO

Dedicated to S. Maria Assunta (St Mary of the Assumption), the cathedral is first mentioned in records dating to 1092. This superb example of northern Italian (Po valley) Romanesque occupies the site of an early-christian era Basilica, the only remains of which are some floor mosaics displayed in the crypt. The church was consecrated in 1106 — the High Middle Ages, a period of political, economic and cultural renaissance in the West. Locally, this reawakening was marked by the construction of the great Romanesque buildings all along the Via Emilia roadway.

As was customary in the Middle Ages, work on the cathedral began with the presbytery sec-

tion. Although an earthquake in 1117 caused some damage, construction was completed by about 1130. Alterations were undertaken almost immediately: from 1160-70, the trussed nave roof was replaced by cross or groin vaults, and towards the end of the 1200s the façade's apex, the lantern, and the upper choir and transept areas were remodelled.

The sandstone façade is accented by two paral-

---

1. Night view of Piazza del Duomo. 2. Duomo. The front is seen from a loggia of Battistero.

2

25

1. Duomo. The apsidal part. 2. Apsidal part, detail of the little loggias. 3. Nave: in front you can see the Verona marble altar of the XII century.

2

lel rows of loggias across it, an arching wall-gallery above these and three portals. The central or main entrance is emphasised by a distyle porch or prothyrum with each column rising from pronelion pedestals. This portal dates to 1281 and is attributed to Giambono da Bissone, who employed an earlier arc carved with depictions of the months symbolised as figures engaged in farm work along the soffit or underside. As was the medieval custom, the calendar begins ab incarnatione on the Annunciation, the 25th of March — a youthful March removing a thorn from his foot, followed by April holding two flowering boughs, May is a knight, June is sharpening a scythe, July reaping, August readying casks, September harvesting grapes, October holding a cup of wine in his right hand, November skinning a pig, December chopping wood, January the two-faced Janus and February the fisherman.

On the left-hand side of the façade is an unfinished tower, possibly of medieval origin, but definitely worked on by the architect Smeraldo Smeraldi in 1602. On the right-hand side is the splendid bell tower or campanile (1284-91). Atop its pinnacle is a copy of the famous 14th-century gilt copper statue of an angel — the original is found inside on the third left-hand pillar of the nave.

Particularly noteworthy inside are the 12th-century animal motifs decorating the apse and transepts, accented in turn by their galleries. These sections of the church were raised in the late 13th century and further altered during the Renaissance. Another peculiarity of the church is the posterior wings added in the late 14th-early 15th centuries to accommodate the transept's east apses (now used as sacristies). The sides of the cathedral were altered in the 13th-14th centuries by the addition of chapels (the south side was not completed until the 19th century). Today the upper half of the nave is all that remains of the Romanesque masonry.

The interior itself has a Latin-cross plan, with the nave set off by banded pillars from the two aisles, featuring galleries and raised presbytery and transepts below which lies the crypt.

THE ROMANESQUE TOUR. Let's begin the tour with the capitals of the nave and the women's galleries, examples of Lombard craftsmanship. The fantastic and grotesque figures depicting the struggle between good and evil retain all the raw expressive power of their age, as do the scenes from the bible, lives of the saints and everyday medieval life portrayed along with them. Note, too, how the figurative elements are balanced with plant motifs.

First capital, right-hand side: The west face (towards the main portal) portrays St Martin encountering the poor man; the north (turning to the left) depicts

the archangels Michael and Gabriel vanquishing the forces of evil; the east (altarward) wild beasts in combat; and the south a pair of gryphons on dragons.

The second capital pictures knights and Saracens in combat, a miniature chronicle of the Crusades. On the fourth capital, south face, are a man and woman picking grapes.

Fourth capital left-hand aisle: the north face shows a scene of baptism by immersion. The third capital features the Sacrifice of Isaac in all its dramatic immediacy. The second capital: On the west face the Virgin enthroned and angels; on the north the Woman of the Apocalypse astride a seven-headed dragon; and on the east is St Nicola of Bari with the three sisters. The first capital: The west face bears the symbols of the four evangelists — the lion for St Mark, the eagle for St John, the ox for St Luke and the angel for St Matthew; the north has an enigmatic scene of a man holding two trees and another beside him armed with a sword; on the east are two lions symbolising good in combat with grotesque basilisks, half-serpent half-cock, symbolising evil; and on the south three angels appearing to Abraham and Sarah.

One final note before coming to the chapels: on the east face of the left-hand gallery's second capital two wolves are depicted in monks' robes — a satyric reference to the practise of simony.

Leitmotifs similar to the ones we have been looking

1. Duomo. Nave: first capital on the right representing the Archangels Michael and Gabriel. 2. Nave: second capital on the right, called «of knights». 3. Nave.

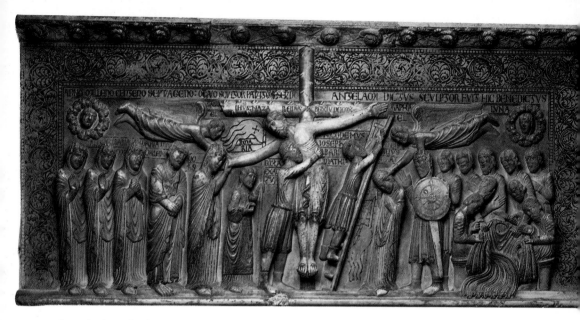

at are also to be found in the outside reliefs and figures.

The fifth chapel on the right: Noteworthy the seven marble tablets recently discovered during restoration of the chancel area. Two show St Martin meeting the poor man and Samson taking a lion by the jaws (*ca.* 1120), both attributed to the sculptor Niccolò. Two others, bearing rosettes on a background of entwining foliage, may have been part of a rood screen. The two with aedicules enclosing a cross could be fragments from an early-christian sarcophagus, while the last, a late-antique rendering of a youth with a basket of fruit on his head, was probably a memorial stone of some sort.

Right transept: Benedetto Antelami's superb high-relief the **Deposizione**, Christ being taken down from the cross. The Latin inscription reads: *«anno milleno centeno septuageno octavo sculptor patuit mense secundo Antelami dictus sculptor fuit hic Benedictus»* (a sculptor was revealed in the second month of the year 1178, this sculptor was Benedict called Antelami).

The relief is dominated by the centre foreground scene of Christ being lowered from the cross by Joseph of Arimathaea on the left and Nicodemus on the right of the ladder. On the far left are depicted the three Marys, St John, the Madonna lifting her son's hand to her cheek and the symbolic figure (the reason it is the smallest) of the Church triumphant holding in her right hand a chalice and in the left the banner of victory. In the foreground on the far right area is the expressively rendered group of Roman soldiers casting lots for Christ's garments; in the background behind them are five male figures representing the Jews, the centurion and, lastly, the symbolic Synagogue vanquished with torn banner.

The tableau culminates horizontally with the two archangels: Gabriel tending the Madonna Christ's hand and Raphael bowing the Synagogue's head. The upper corners feature the male head of the sun, left, and the female moon's, right, in foliar wreathes. A finely wrought niello-work edging and rose-pattern frame on the upper protruding border frame the Deposition.

The relief's compositional symmetry is heightened by the oblique tension of the central figures: the skewed angles of the Christ and the Synagogue on the right are countered by the opposite-leaning figures of Joseph and Nicodemus. The group of animated soldiers adds an anecdotal touch. A recent theory has even been advanced identifying the scene as the «mystical union of Christ the bridegroom with the Church, the newly-wedded spouse that issued from the wound in his side, and the repudiation of the Synagogue seen as the former bride».

This is one of the great masterpieces of Romanesque sculpture. It bears clear traces of classical art and the unmistakable influences of the Provençal school, with which Antelami presumably had contact, although the arrangement and monumental rendering of his figures are quite original. The existence of another tablet (irretrieveably worn), three capitals (in the Galleria Nazionale), four lions-base columns (against the rear façade) and two Atlantes or Telamones (first chapel on right) would seem to suggest that the Deposition formed with these other works part of a chancel arch or pulpit.

This chancel arch or rood screen was demolished in 1566 during the Counter-Reformation by Girolamo Mazzola Bedoli, who replaced it with the staircase in red Verona marble.

The «**Cattedra Vescovile**» or bishop's cathedra in the choir is also by Antelami. The sides of the chair, resting on two seated animals, portray St George kill-

1. Duomo. Right part of the transept. Benedetto Antelami: La Deposizione (1178). 2. Detail of the Deposizione with Christ on the cross in the middle, Giuseppe d'Arimatea and the triumphing Church on the left-hand, Nicodemo and the defeated Synagogue on the right-hand.

ing the dragon on the left and the conversion of St Paul on the right. The arm-rests are in the form of ornately carved lions supported by two Atlantes.

At the centre of the presbytery or chancel is the high altar of red and white Verona marble. Executed by craftsmen in the late 12th century, it features a vesica or «mandorla» (upright almond shape) of Christ with tetramorph (composite figure combining the symbols of the four evangelists), Sts Abdom and Sennen amid lions, nine apostles, St Bartholomew (added later) and the decapitation of the two martyrs.

The crypt. It still conforms to its original plan, despite the alterations in the 16th and 17th centuries. The numerous columns emphasising the space vary in size and were originally part of pre-existing buildings. Their Corinthian capitals date to the early 12th century, when the church was built.

THE RENAISSANCE TOUR. Throughout the 1500s, radical alterations were undertaken to embellish the Duomo. The vaults and walls were covered with frescos, endowing them with an entirely different appearance.

In 1522 Correggio (Antonio Allegri, ca. 1489-1534) was commissioned to execute the fresco of the cupola or dome. If you look on the north arch, you will see a bust figure of the prophet Zachary, all that remains of one of the pre-existing decorations done in the 1400s. Although the remodelling of the dome itself was carried out by the architect Giorgio da Erba, the design was probably the work of Correggio, who doubtlessly planned the eight large oculi or circular openings in the drum or dome's midsection.

Precursor of the dynamic skies so characteristic of the Baroque by more than a century, Correggio completed this masterpiece of the fresco from 1526-30. Its

theme is the **Assumption**, perhaps reflecting the special veneration Parma then had for the Virgin. The subject also is a reaffirmation of the Catholic faith in the face of the iconoclastic polemics stirred by Luther's Reform at the time. On the drum, before the illusionistic balustra (trompe l'œil), the apostles are caught in expressions of animated surprise by the miracle taking place above their heads. In a spatial vortex without end, the Virgin is assumed into heaven, as if raised by the host of frenetic and voluptuous angels beneath, while her son descends from on high towards her.

The pendentives bear naturalistically rendered conches or sea-shells on which are depicted the city's four patrons: Sts Bernard, John the Baptist, Ilario and a figure that has traditionally been recognised as Thomas but that a recent study has identified as St Joseph. The arches feature an ornate frieze with putti and plants volutes, and their bases are decorated with six monochrome figures of comely youths.

Correggio left the fresco unfinished. The east arch was done by Girolamo Mazzola Bedoli, who also finished the rest of the sanctuary and the Last Judgement on the apse ceiling that were part of Correggio's commission. His abrupt departure was probably due to misunderstandings with the church's trustees, who could not or would not accept the artist's revolutionary pictorial techniques. Correggio was one of the first to use the Sotto in sù (literally below upwards) meaning an extreme illusionistic perspective depicting figures painted on a ceiling so foreshortened as to appear floating in space above the spectator.

Girolamo Mazzola Bedoli was a second-generation Parmesan mannerist, whose other works include the decoration of the nave's vaults and lunettes, 1555-57. The vast wall frescos portraying scenes from the life of Christ and culminating in the rear-façade's imposing Resurrection are the work of Lattanzio Gambara of Brescia and his helper, Bernardino Gatti of Cremona. They were done from 1567 to 1573.

The vaults of the aisles, featuring the figures of putti and flowers, were frescoed by Alessandro Mazzola Bedoli, Girolamo's son, between 1571-74. The upper right-hand transept groin vault was originally decorated by Michelangelo Anselmi in the 1500s. The fresco began to disintegrate and was reworked in the 18th century by Antonio Bresciani. The north groin vault's fresco was painted by the Bolognese artist, Orazio Samacchini, 1570-74.

OTHER VALUABLE WORKS. Beginning on the right, the first chapel houses the Visitation, late 15th-early 16th centuries, painted by Cristoforo Caselli. The fourth or so-called «Comune» chapel is frescoed with scenes from the lives of Sts Sebastian and Fabian. Together with the fresco decoration of the fifth and chronologically earlier «Valeri» chapel on the left, it is attributed to Bartolino de' Grossi, first-half of the 15th century. These works show the Lombard stylis-

1

1. Duomo. Detail of the dome by Correggio: pendentive with S. Giovanni Battista. 2. Correggio. The great fresco of the dome representing the Ascension of the Virgin.

tic predilections for background perspectives and heightening of everyday details. The «Comune» chapel's scenes are rhythmically more pondered than the «Valeri's» yet both display close stylistic affinities in the physiognomy and expressiveness of the figures and the sturdy, quotidien plastic values informing them. The pala or altarpiece of the Madonna and Child with saints, ca. 1526, is by Michelangelo Anselmi.

The fifth chapel has a 1516 Virgin and Child between Sts Anthony and Paul by Alessandro Araldi (oil on canvas), and Francesco Maria Rondani's wall frescos (1527-31) depicting (above) scenes of the Passion and, on the socle or base, monochrome episodes from the life of St Anthony, abbot. The last chapel on the right, St Agatha's, is decorated with the superb frescos of Sebastiano Galeotti, who executed the figures, and Pellegrino Spaggiari, who did the quadrature or illusionist decorations (1719). On the altar is Bernardino Gatti's pala (1566-74) portraying the Crucified Christ attended by Mary Magdalene, St Agatha and St Bernardo degli Uberti.

Right-hand transept. On the walls leading up into the transept are two large paintings, a King David and St Cecilia, by E.C. Procaccini.

Cappella Montini. The Montini chapel was frescoed in 1506-07 by Cristoforo Caselli and features the figure of God the Father along with painted mosaic decoration (false mosaics). On the left is the tomb of the canon Bartolomeo Montini; the pictorial part was executed by Caselli and the sculpture by Giovan Francesco D'Agrate.

Cappella di San Paolo. St Paul's chapel contains the pala, Conversion of St Paul, painted by Antonio Bresciani in 1796.

Sagrestia «dei Consorziali». Entered through a small door to the right of the choir, the **sacristy** contains wood furnishings (1488) by Cristoforo Canozzi da Lendinara, who also began the intarsia benchwork finished by Luchino Bianchino, whose work also includes the Duomo's entry doors (1494). Emphasised by lesenes inlaid with grotesque-work, the backs display intarsia-composed perspective views. The bottom mirrors feature a series of geometric shapes that rigorously adhere to the dictates of perspective as espoused by Piero della Francesca, whom Lendinara and his son had come into contact. The large central bench was executed, in fact, by both Cristoforo and his son, Bernardino. The father also executed the wooden **choir** round the presbytery walls. Signed and dated 1473, it comprises twenty top and bottom stalls with volute-inlay arm-rests and perspective intarsiae of objects and alternating landscapes.

Left-hand transept, the Cappella dell'Assunta. The chapel of the Assumption contains Giovan Battista Tinti's pala (1589), and, left, two organ doors bearing the images of two knights by E.C. Procaccini.

Also noteworthy is the large painting that features Christ Crucified and various Franciscan saints by Gaspare Traversi, 1753, along the stairway.

The **Crypt**. Once in the crypt, a door in the right-hand wall of the central chapel leads to the Rusconi chapel. Completed in 1417, it was dedicated to St John by Giovanni Rusconi, Bishop of Parma, whose figure is on the right as you enter, next to the Virgin enthroned and Sts John the Evangelist and John the Baptist. Variously framed all round the vault are the busts of prophets, kings and patriarchs. Although the artist is anonymous, certain formal refinements of the fresco bear the strong imprint of the Lombard Gothic

hile others show the influence of Trecento-Veneto
rt (1300's), especially marked in the elaborate archi-
ectonic structure of the throne that closely resembles
hose in the two Incoronazioni (coronations) by Al-
chiero at Padua.

The floor of the central chapel contains two mosaic
ragments that were discovered in the Piazza of the
Duomo in 1955. It is believed that one belonged to the
'omus ecclesiae or clergy house and the other, with its
antharus or drinking cup design bordered by sym-
olic fish-like motifs, to the early-christian basilica.
he altar is adorned with a painting of St Ilario (1733)
y Antonio Balestra.

Opposite the Rusconi chapel is that named for the
anon Antonio Ravacaldi, who had it built in the early
5th century and decorated with frescos depicting
cenes from the life of the Virgin by an anonymous
ombard artist. On the right as you enter is Joachim's
ision of the angel announcing the Virgin's birth. Left,
he Presentation of Mary in the Temple, followed by
he Betrothal and, on the back wall, the Annunciation
ith members of the Ravacaldi family depicted there-
. Marked by the courtly Gothic of their linear com-
osition, the scenes succeed one another with a fluid
race while the figures are heightened by a command-
g expressiveness.

We next come upon the work of two important ex-
onents of local 16th-century painting: the Betrothal
f the Virgin (1519-20) by Alessandro Araldi, and the
526 St Agnes appearing to members of her family by
ichelangelo Anselmi.

The Valeri Chapel. The fifth chapel in the left-hand
isle on leaving the crypt, it is polygonal in form and
ecorated throughout by the early 15th-century
othic frescos attributed to Bartolino de' Grossi of
arma. Against the sky-blue background of the fan

vault in gilded «tondi» or circles are painted eight
scenes from the life of the Virgin. The wall panels depict events in the lives of Sts Andrew Apostle, Catherine and Christopher drawn from the book Legenda
Aurea («Golden Legend»). The episodes, faced-
paced and crowded with figures, are in the Lombard
style. They were originally accompanied by captions
in Gothic lettering that have all but vanished today.
The human likenesses, local types delineated with animated features emphasising their air of 14th-century
sanguine earthiness, are depicted within rather con-
fining settings. The Lombard penchant for natural detail can be seen in the small animal figures informing
the decoration. Noteworthy, too, is the Death of
Christ, in the niche, painted by an anonymous local
artist of the 1400s.

The second chapel. The walls are adorned by four
Gaspare Traversi paintings executed in 1753: Sts Lu-
cia, Agatha and Apollonia; St Anthony of Padua; St
Peter; and saints adoring the eucharist.

*Duomo. The late fifteenth-century sacristy of Consorziali,
egun by Cristoforo da Lendinara and finished by Luchino
ianchino. 2. Crypt. Ruins of the mosaic flooring of the an-
ent early Christian basilica. 3. Crypt. Rusconi Chapel.. San
iovanni Battista. 4. Crypt. Rusconi Chapel. Musician An-
el. 5. Crypt. Ravacaldi Chapel. Annunciation Angel.*

1. Duomo. Valery Chapel. Sant'Andrea's tales. 2. Valery Chapel. The vault. 3. Valery Chapel. San Cristoforo's tales. 4. Valery Chapel. Detail of the eastern wall.

THE BATTISTERO

The Baptistry is Italy's most complex and exciting medieval monument. As to its origin, the Latin inscription above the north portal's architrave lets the mute stones speak: *«bis binis demptis annis de mille ducentis incepit dictus opus hoc sculptor Benedictus»* or «twice two years before 1200 the sculptor Benedict doth begin this work». The year is 1196 and the sculptor is Benedetto Antelami, whose first work, the marble Deposition (1178) in the Duomo, proclaims that he is also an architect belonging to the Guild of the Antelami from the Intelvi valley.

The exterior is an octagon, a symbolic number according to medieval tradition. One of the several meanings it encompasses is that which states that the number eight signifies the eighth day of creation, that is, the new creation that began with the resurrection of Christ and is continued in the sacrament of baptism. To facilitate the supply of water needed for its liturgical function, it was built over the city's main canal, which also served to transport the valuable pink Verona marble that covers it directly to the site.

This superb prism is divided into eight faces with salient (protruding) corners rising to as many lanterns and features three — north, west and south — splayed portals. Its exterior mass is emphasised by four tiers of loggias with architrave that are crowned by pointed blind arches.

Work progressed under Antelami's stewardship until 1216, when building was suspended at an advanced stage due to a breakdown in relations with Verona, supplier of the marble revetment. Work recommenced in 1259 and the building was completed in 1270.

As we look at the Baptistry in detail, it's a good idea to keep in mind that the pictorial representations on exterior and interior alike are intimately connected by a unifying iconography or meaning.

THE NORTH PORTAL. Giving on to the piazza or square, it features a lunette above which are the archangels Michael and Gabriel and in which is a tableau scene depicting the **Madonna enthroned and Child** flanked on the left by the three Magi being guided by an angel and on the right by St Joseph's dream preceding the flight into Egypt. The intrados or soffit (underside) of the arch bears the figures of the twelve major prophets each holding a clypeus or round shield depicting one of the twelve apostles. On the architrave, from the left, are detailed the baptism

2

of Christ, Herod's banquet at which Salomè asks for the head of John the Baptist and the saint's decapitation.

Left door-jamb: From bottom to top is portrayed the geneology of Christ culminating with the figure of Moses, his prefiguration. Right door-jamb: The geneological tree of the Virgin. The internal door-jambs are adorned with the *Peridexion* or Tree of Life on whose branches perch doves and souls that are protected, left, by cocks and priests, and threatened on the right by dragons or evil.

The dominant iconographic theme of the portal's motifs is the Old Testament's role as precursor through the prophets, who preached the coming of the Saviour, of the New Testament. This is pointedly brought to the fore by the juxtapositions of statues in the niche on the left of David and Isaiah, who foretold the adoration of the Magi or wise men from the East at Christ's birth, and the two figures in the niche on the right of the Queen of Sheba coming to King Solomon, an analogous foreshadowing of the New Testament event. The architrave scenes from the life of the Baptist are in homage to St John, the Baptistry's patron.

THE WEST PORTAL. It features the first sculptural representation in Italy of the **Last Judgement**. In the centre of the lunette is a seated Christ showing his wounds; on the backs of his hands can be seen the clover design, symbol of the Trinity; the angels about him bear the objects of the Passion. The small seated figure on the left is St Paul. On the arch's soffit are two groups of apostles divided in the middle by two clarion angels. The resurrection of the dead is portrayed

---

1. Via Cardinal Ferrari with the Battistero on the background, on the right-hand the southern side of the Duomo and on the left-hand the Palazzo del Seminario Maggiore. 2. Battistero. Northern Portal.

1. Battistero. Benedetto Antelami. Lunette of the northern portal devoted to the Virgin. 2. Western Portal. 3. Benedetto Antelami. Lunette of the western portal with the Last Judgement. 4. Detail of the lunette with St. Paul and Angels. 5. Southern Portal. 6. Details of the southern lunette with Apollo and the tree of life. 7. Detail of the southern lunette with Diana.

CITE OFFICI BET TOBE FERDITE (OZE?)

5

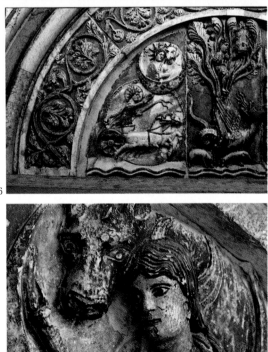

6

7

on the architrave: the serenity of the elect on the left contrasts sharply with the shame of the damned covering their nakedness on the right. Antelami's genius of invention can be seen in the door-jambs where the path to heaven is illustrated with the six works of mercy on the left, and the parable of the grape vine according to the Gospel of St Mathew on the right.

THE SOUTH PORTAL. The decorative motif here is drawn from the oriental tale of **Barlaam and Josephat** that enjoyed wide currency in the Middle Ages. A young boy is gathering honey from a beehive in a tree being gnawed by two rodents while a dragon with jaws agape menaces him from above. On his left are the figures of Apollo, the sun, and Diana, the moon — symbols of time's ceaseless day and night passage. The boy (humanity) is so absorbed in the pursuit of worldly pleasure (honey) that he loses track of time and is oblivious to the perils threatening his very existence (dragon, rodents). The arch's soffit is adorned with a delicate foleat volute, while the architrave features clypeus-figures of Christ flanked by the Lamb of God and John the Baptist.

The Baptistry is girded round by a zoophorus, a frieze of animal reliefs on a series of marble panels, recalling the medieval beastiary — here rendered less terrifying in the clearly wrought circles and squares.

Although the imposing mass of the Baptistry is still Romanesque in style, its pictorial decorations denote the influence of the new Gothic from beyond the Alps, especially northern

41

France. This is most clearly seen in the prominence accorded the Virgin — the main portal is dedicated to her — and the changed representational mode for Christ — from the severe judge of the Romanesque portals to the Gothic's more human figure, sign of a new religious mentality. There is to be noted, too, the development in Antelami's style from the rigidity of the gestures and garments in the Deposition of twenty years earlier to the greater fluidity of the figures of the Baptistry.

The south's portal's lunette is a good example of this enhanced plasticity of the figures — the fleeting Apollo and Diana, the rustling of the branches and the demonic twisting of the dragon about the tree. The effect is heightened by the original polychromy that current restoration has brought to light.

The interior. The octagon exterior becomes a 16-sided polygon, with each side rising in Gothic exuberance to form the rose-coloured marble webs of the crowning umbrella dome.

The scenes on the reverse side of the three portals' lunettes complement those depicted on the outside: the north has the *Flight into Egypt* backing Joseph's dream; the west *David*, prefiguration of Christ, playing the psalter amid musicians and dancers; and south the first appearance in Romanesque Lombard sculpture of the *Presentation in the Temple*, a foreshadowing of the baptism that arms the neophyte against the snares of the world so graphically depicted as the youth in the tree on the outside.

At the east end, in observance of canon tradition, is the pink Verona marble high altar, decorated with the Baptist flanked by a priest and a Levite. The lunette features a vesica or **mandorla** of Christ framed by the tetramorph or figure combining the symbols of the four evangelists. In the other lunettes are isolated figures of angels in various poses as well as an Annunciation.

The centre is occupied by the large, tub-like immersion baptismal font hewed from a single stone block (late 13th century).

1. Battistero. Niche on the right of the northern portal. Detail of the Queen of Saba. 2. Detail of the zoophorus. 3. Detail of the zoophorus. 4. The interior. Workers. Northern lunette with the flight into Egypt. 5. Benedetto Antelami. Western lunette with David playing psaltery among musicians and dancers.

4

To the right of the south portal is the small, asper-
ion font. It rests on a crouching lion, symbol of evil,
clutching a helpless hare, the soul. The font itself actually crushes the lion symbolising the lustral water's
victory over evil. The Peridexion or tree of life decorative motif includes souls being threatened by basilisks.

The sculptures of the **months** and **seasons** are for
the first time rendered monumentally, elevating the
labours of man to a new dignity. March sounds the oli-
phant or ivory horn, symbol of ancient farming traditions; May is a knight bearing a scythe, a symbol combining chivalry and labour; June reaps, July threshes,
August prepares the casks, September picks the
grapes, October sows, November pulls up the turnips,
December chops wood, January's two-faced Janus
warms himself by the hearth and February hoes the
field.

Several of the stone steles portray the signs of the
zodiac; the rest are part of the first gallery's walls. Two
seasons complete the cycle: **Winter**, left, naked and
with a leafy branch behind him symbolising the still
mild autumn and, right, cloaked and with a bare
branch behind him signifying the season's rigours; and

*1. Battistero. The interior. Benedetto Antelami. Southern lu-
nette with the Presentation in the Temple. 2. Workers. Eastern
lunette with Christ among the symbols of the four Evangelists.
3. Workers. The month of October. 4. Workers. Winter. 5.
Workers. Spring.*

5

pring — one of Italian sculpture's most distinctive
orks of this transitional epoch from the Roma-
esque to the Gothic — depicted as a slender, elegant-
attired maiden with a flower diadem holding her
air in place.

Only the interior's south and west lunette decora-
ons can with certainty be attributed to Antelami; the
est were executed by craftsmen working from his de-
gns. The expansiveness of the figures in their spatial
ontext and the naturalness of their gestures mark
ese works as being later than those decorating the
xterior.

The Cupola. The dome's vertical rise is divided
to four bays superbly adorned by unifying frescos (c.
260-70) bearing the mark of Byzantine origin.
bout the boss or keystone is a star-punctuated red
y set off by a geometric frame motif of stars heigh-
ned by shading against a green background. The sec-
d bay, it too with the frame motif, portrays the apos-
es and the symbols of the four evangelists to east and
est. In the third is a Deësis, a group of Christ en-
roned with the Virgin and St John on either side, fol-
wed by the prophets. The last has twelve panels por-
aying the life of St John the Baptist and the remain-
er depicting figures of the saints. Beginning from the
ft of the west portal, the first scene is the annuncia-
on of the Baptist's birth to Zacharias and Elisabeth,
llowed by his birth, an angel leading the youthful
ohn into the desert, his sermon, St John baptizing,
ohn presenting Jesus to the people, the baptism of
hrist, the Baptist brought before Herod, two of
ohn's disciples, the miracles of Christ before the
aptist's disciples, the feast of Herod.

The tempera paintings adorning the archways and
ost of the lunettes that already had Antelami's sculp-
res in place were also executed by the Byzantine
aftsmen. They were probably called in to complete
ecorations that were left unfinished when work was
alted in 1216. Traces of the earlier paintings can still
e seen in the lunette above the altar and in the second
nette to the left of the entrance that bears the fresco
two stylized young trees.

Excepting the fresco depicting the Baptism of
hrist behind the altar, which is contemporary with
e cupola decorations, all the others in the lower
ches date to the 14th century and are votive works.
rticularly noteworthy is the Gothic fresco to the left
the central niche. It portrays Bishop Gerardo Bian-
i (d. 1302) kneeling before the Virgin enthroned
d flanked by the Baptist and an angel.

The fresco in the niche to the right of the centre one
the work of a sole artist commissioned by the Chapel

2

or society for the Living and the Dead. Dating to 1399,
it features, above, Christ crucified amid saints and
mourners and, below, Our Lady of Mercy and the
faithful embraced by her mantle.

To the right of the south portal are frescos of St
George and the dragon and St Catherine, attributed
by critics to Buffalmacco (the nickname derives from
Boccaccio's Decameron), the artist of the Trionfo della Morte («Triumph of Death») at Pisa's Camposanto
(cemetery). Completed ca. 1330-36, they evince his
stylistic peculiarities, i.e. heightened Gothic delinea-
tion, carefully detailed clothing and, most typically,
the rendering of his figures' eyes emphasised by a
marked shadow effect.

PALAZZO VESCOVILE

Until its commissioning outside the walls in
1055 by Count Cadalo, the bishop, the seat of the
bishopric had always been within the fortifications. Alterations have since changed its aspect a
number of times.

The first date to the 12th century and are still
evident in the north side and the north-west tower or keep. In 1232-34, Bishop Grazia had the
architect Rolandello enlarge it and add porticoes
and three-light mullion windows to the façade.
The inner gallery was built and the façade's porticoes were walled to create additional rooms in
the 15th century. The early 16th century wit-
nessed the transformation of some mullion into
rectangular windows and the addition of the terracotta cornice.

The palazzo's present-day appearance is the
result of 20th-century restoration that revived
the medieval and Renaissance elements by elimi-
nating the 18th-century facelift.

PALAZZO DEL SEMINARIO

Built shortly after the Duomo, the seminary
was originally connected at one end to the former's south side by a cloister, which ran the
length of the present-day Via Cardinal Ferrari,
and at the other to the town walls. The cloister

Battistero. The interior. Byzantine workers. The dome. 2.
reat niche on the right of the northern portal. Fresco with St.
eorge and the drake and St. Catherine probably by Buffal-
acco.

47

was demolished in 1513 to provide direct access to the newly erected Church of St John.

In 1516, it became a Gymnasium or grammar school and a public library. The façade designed by Giovan Francesco d'Agrate also dates to this period. In 1566, the diocesan seminary replaced the Gymnasium and has been there ever since. The closing of the portico and gallery above it was completed in the 17th century.

SAN GIOVANNI EVANGELISTA

The present-day Church of St John the Evangelist was erected in a fifty-year span beginning in the late 1400s. It belongs to the Benedictines, as did the original monastery (ca. 980) that it replaces, which was destroyed by fire during one of the frequent outbreaks of violence between feuding factions of the local nobility.

From its founding in the Middle Ages, the monastery had an important impact on the city. That influence stemmed from its charity works and cultural patronage. The Benedictines set up hospitals, xenodochia or hospices for strangers and even a public pharmacy. And, together with the other Benedictine houses in the city, St John's

became one of the leading exponents of Parma Humanism and among the keenest and mos knowledgeable patrons of Renaissance art — er deavours that often made the Order a rival of th noble courts themselves.

While the actual building was done under th supervision first of Giliolo da Reggio (1490 1519) and thereafter of Bernardino Zaccagni o Parma, the Benedictines themselves were direc ly involved in all phases of the work. In all likel hood, they also designed the church, as St John is one of the city's first Renaissance style edifice

There were two exceptions. The Baroque façad (1604-07), which was designed by the duke's arch tect Simone Moschino, erected by Giovan Battis Carra da Bissone (to whom the statues of the Order saints and abbots adorning it are attributed) an crowned by the imposing copper eagle, symbol of th evangelist. And the bell tower or campanile, whic dates to 1618 and is attributed to Giovan Battis Magnani of Parma.

The Latin-cross interior plan features a nave d vided from the side aisles by cruci-form pillars, groit vault ceilings and a dome surmounting the crossing o the nave, chancel and transepts. The aisles are punctu ated by six, polygonal-plan chapels, and the chance flanked by two more.

While it has much in common with the Rom: nesque Duomo, St John's has numerous points of co tact with the emergent Renaissance architecture. Pe haps this is best expressed in the pillars and chape Of grey stone with fluted shafts and finely wrough composite-order capitals the pillars are clearly mo delled on those by Brunelleschi in the Church of Lorenzo — just as the festoon-work on the capitals the three pillars nearest the apse recalls that by Alber in the Tempio Malatestiano at Rimini. Unlike the D omo, the chapels on either side of the chancel are pe fectly aligned to the aisles and in keeping with the ne concept of perspective. The influence of the stylist innovations is even more readily apparent in the d corations than in the architecture per se, as we sha see in Correggio's cupola.

The first of these interior adornments is the larg Vision of St John on the island of Patmos (1687), c the inside front wall, by the Genoese artist Giova Battista Merano. On the pillars to the left, tablets con memorating Parma's most distinguished humanis point to the monastery's outstanding cultural role the 14-1500s.

The groin vaults and arches of the nave were deco ated with their candelabras, putti and symbols of th church's patron saint about 1520 by the painte

1

1. Church of San Giovanni Evangelista. The Baroque fro was planned by Simone Moschino. 2. Nave.

Michelangelo Anselmi of Siena. Having come to Parma sometime between 1516-20, he played a decisive role as go-between in bringing Tuscan Mannerism to Parma.

The grotesques or fanciful ornamental decorations on the pilasters are by Correggio (1522-23). They are characterized by a fullness that is almost Baroque, a style which did much to revive this ornamental motif. Correggio's, too, is the frieze running along the nave's walls that extends the one done by others on the transept, although his rendering of the sacrifice theme is christian rather than pagan. The frieze, with the alternating repetition of its central monochrome motif, depicts the Sacrifice of the Lamb and the Altar of the God Unknown. These scenes, which are completely lacking of any historical reference, stand as generic representations of worship that appear to exalt a universal religion. The scenes are enclosed by figures of the Prophets (Latin inscriptions) and Sybils (Greek inscriptions) illustrating the life of Christ. Does the repetition of both the monochrome episodes and the pilasters' grotesques presuppose the almost certain use of cartoons (detailed full-size drawings ready for transfer to canvas, walls, panels) and, hence, the assistance of others in executing Correggio's designs? If so, Francesco Maria Rondani of Parma was undoubtedly among them.

All the vaults and walls of the aisle chapels were redecorated from 1667-1730. Save the fourth chapels on left and right, both frescoed by Merano, the baroque flair for figures and illusionistic prospectives was fashioned by fresco masters working in pairs – Angelo Michele Colonna and Giacomo Alboresi initially and Giacomo Antonio Boni and Tommaso Aldovrandini thereafter — all of whom were from Bologna. A local artist, Giuseppe Carpi, was also involved.

The right-hand chapels. Noteworthy is the oil on wood Nativity (1519) in the second one by the Bolognese brothers Giacomo and Giulio Francia, and the altarpiece or «pala» Adoration of the Magi (1499) in the third by Cristoforo Caselli of Parma, who was influenced by Venetian painting, as can be seen in the minutely depicted journey scene (upper part). Apart from the frescos portraying episodes in the life of St James painted by the above-mentioned Merano in 1684, the fourth chapel boasts a Madonna and Child with St James Major (1542-43) by Girolamo Bedoli Mazzola, an artist of Parma's second Mannerism with close ties to Parmigianino, whose name he wished to assume after having married one of the latter's cousins. The fifth chapel, too, merits attention — it contains works by Correggio executed after 1524 and commissioned by the Del Bono family. Two are paintings: a Deposition and the Martyrdom of Four Saints both 18th-century copies of the originals on display in the National Gallery. The under-arch or soffit fresco depicting God the Father flanked by Sts Peter and Andrew on the right and St Paul falling from his horse on the left is also attributed to Correggio.

Right transept, St John's Chapel. This saint was the monastery's first abbot, and his remains are preserved in an urn under the ornate late 17th-century altar, while scenes from his life are depicted in the vault frescos painted by Anselmi in 1521. The altarpiece of the Miracle of St Benedict is by the Bolognese artist Emilio Taruffi and dates to about 1674.

The transept walls are background to the finely wrought statues of St Felicity and her son, Vitalis, with St Benedict. They were executed in 1543 by the Modenese sculptor Antonio Begarelli, who also did the other statues in the left transept of St John the Evangelist and the Madonna and Child with St Giovannino. Covered with a coat of white to simulate marble, all the figures are terracotta. They originally adorned the dormitory until being removed here in the 1800s.

Righthand presbitery chapel. Noteworthy is the fine fresco under the arch of St Cecilia at the organ and St Margaret and the dragon. Until its recent attribution to Bedoli, this fresco had been ascribed at various times to him, Parmigianino and Anselmi — a tribute to the stylistic affinities linking these three exponents of local Mannerism.

Below the transept arch runs a frieze featuring tondi or circular pictures portraying perspective busts of popes, bishops and Benedictine monks interposed by monochrome scenes of sacrificial rites repeated with only the slightest variations. Yet the stylistic differences between the right and left walls are clearly evident. The latter part is dated 1514 and signed by an otherwise unknown artist, Giovanni Antonio da Parma, while the former is of clearly superior quality and seems to resemble especially in the **tondi** the bronze plaques produced at Padua in the 1400s.

The **cupola**. One of Correggio's masterpieces the dome's fresco art is the first work he executed

1

he church (1520) and beyond doubt the most impressive in terms of innovative and powerful illusionistic concept. With its Baroque-like style acting as a prelude to the fully developed swirling vortex of sky and figures in the Duomo's cupola, the frescos show Correggio breaking through the physical bounds of the walls by architecting the illusion of space unfettered — an open sky upon whose clouds are posed the apostles drawn with a Michelangeloesque plasticity and vigour and the central figure of Christ seen in the sotto in su or from below upwards perspective.

Iconographically speaking, the subject depicted is almost as complex in meaning as the technique that created it. At first glance it appears to be an Ascension of Christ. But a closer look at the way his robes lift upwards suggests that he is descending not ascending, and the figure of St John, almost hidden on the cornice below the ring of the apostles and visible only from the presbytery, further intimates that the meaning is rather linked to the church's patron saint. The traditional

interpretation as the evangelist's dream on the island of Patmos has recently been upheld in the identification of the subject as St John in Transit — he is portrayed as an old rather than young man «almost poised over the vast tomb represented by the dome's empty space below», while the apostles are leaning towards him and Christ approaches the ground to accompany him upwards.

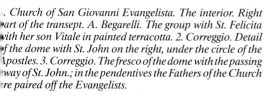

. Church of San Giovanni Evangelista. The interior. Right part of the transept. A. Begarelli. The group with St. Felicita with her son Vitale in painted terracotta. 2. Correggio. Detail of the dome with St. John on the right, under the circle of the Apostles. 3. Correggio. The fresco of the dome with the passing way of St. John.; in the pendentives the Fathers of the Church are paired off the Evangelists.

Portrayed on the pendentives are the Church Fathers and the authors of the Holy Scriptures, while along the drum are the monochrome symbols amid angels of the evangelists. Correggio decorated the arch soffits with monochrome figures of biblical heroes and the semi-pillars beneath with grotesques.

The presbytery. Correggio painted the transept grotesques above the chancel, whereas the putti in the cells or webs of the vault are a later addition.

When the apse was enlarged to its imposing present-day proportions in the 1600s, a frieze by Correggio was partially destroyed. Completed shortly before the one in the nave, it ran along the sanctuary walls and was thematically part of the sacrifice motif. A fragment is on display in the «Sala Capitolare» or Chapter (capitulary) Room, Chapterhouse.

The choir. A superb example of the wood worker's art, it includes 41 upper and 28 lower stalls adorned with intaglio and intarsia inlays depicting city — and landscapes, fruit, musical instruments, books and details of clockworks. The choir was begun in 1512 by Marcantonio Zucchi of Parma and finished in 1538 by the brothers Gianfrancesco and Pasquale Testa.

Two other works are also worthy of note in the apse. One is Bedoli's large 1556 altarpiece of the Transfiguration, strongly derivative of Raphael's painting of the same subject in the Vatican Pinacoteca (museum). The other is the fresco of the Virgin enthroned surrounded by the four Evangelists and Sts Mauro, Benedict and John the Baptist (1686) by the Bolognese artist, Cesare Aretusi. It is a copy of Correggio's fresco (1522) that had adorned the vault before the apse was enlarged and rebuilt. Although there are errors in the perspective at the sides, the copy is an early example of preservative restoration and was undertaken at a time of renewed interest and study of Correggio's works. Of the original fresco, all that remains is the central group depicting Christ and the Virgin on display in the National Gallery, while the sinopia or its underdrawing of reddish-brown colour is in the Biblioteca Palatina («Palatine Library»).

Transept, left presbytery chapel. Noteworthy is the fine underarch or soffit fresco depicting St Agnes, left, and St Catherine, right. Executed by Anselmi in 1522-23, it strongly recalls Parmigianino's mannerist style.

The sacristy. Above its entrance is Correggio's famous lunette fresco of St John writing or, as the inscription reads, «revealing better than any other the divine mysteries».

End transept wall, Chapel of Sts Maurus and Benedict. Decorated, as the chapel directly opposite, by Anselmi in 1521, it features a fresco of St Benedict enthroned with Sts Flavia, Placidus, Maurus and Scolastica. The altarpiece of St Maurus healing plague victims (1674) is by Emilio Taruffi.

Lefthand chapels. In the sixth is the fine oil on wood painting (ca. 1525) of Christ bearing the cross by Anselmi. It is a prime example of the artist's style — the breadth or sweep of the scene, the fully chromatic compositional technique and the predominance of red. The soffit or underarch frescos are probably by Anselmi, too.

The fourth chapel is one of the most impressive for its wealth of decoration. The soffit fresco, one of three by Parmigianino (Francesco Mazzola) in St John's (all

ca. 1522), portrays in niches two bishop saints, Nicola of Bari, right, and Hilary, left. The figures are formally expansive and monumental, still a far cry from the allusive, delicate subtlety of his mature work. The Baroque wall frescos portray, as previously mentioned scenes from St Nicola's life by Merano, and the outstanding altarpiece painting of St Catherine's mystical union (1536) is by Bedoli.

The third chapel is noted for the painting of the Virgin and Child with Sts Stephan (pope) and John the Baptist by the Flemish artist J. Sons, who worked a Parma in the late 1500s.

In the second chapel, the soffit or underarch fresco is also by Parmigianino. It portrays, right, St Vitalis or St Secundus holding back a horse that is illusionistically projecting beyond the scene's confines and, left two deacons reading.

The soffit fresco in the first chapel is again by Parmigianino and was probably the last of the three to be completed. It depicts St Agatha and her executioner and the Sts Apollonia and Lucia. While the righthand figures still retain a certain harshness recalling Pordenone, those on the left clearly have a delicate bearing that recalls, as do the splendid putti along the band Correggio, who was then at work only a few steps from these chapels.

The **sacristy**. The fresco decorations were executed in 1508 by Cesare Cesariano of Milan, celebrated for his Italian translation of Vitruvius. Iconographically speaking, they feature grotesques, emblem figures on the vault groins representing the virtues, cartouches or scroll-work, tondi or circular pictures with biblical scenes in the arches below, and tondi with simulated-marble figures of the virtues on the ceiling

he faces of the virtues are fine examples of the work's
articular stylistic achievement — the «sfumato» tech-
que, meaning the colour or tone transitions from
ght to dark in stages so gradual as to be imperceptible
· that is a hallmark of Leonardo da Vinci in particular
d the period's Milanese school in general.

Also worthy of note are the reliquary cabinet's two
oors decorated by Anselmi in the octagonal annex
lded on to the sacristy in 1618, and the sacristy's fine
ood-work that was executed by local artisans in the
500s.

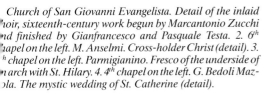

*Church of San Giovanni Evangelista. Detail of the inlaid
hoir, sixteenth-century work begun by Marcantonio Zucchi
nd finished by Gianfrancesco and Pasquale Testa. 2. 6th
hapel on the left. M. Anselmi. Cross-holder Christ (detail). 3.
h chapel on the left. Parmigianino. Fresco of the underside of
n arch with St. Hilary. 4. 4th chapel on the left. G. Bedoli Maz-
la. The mystic wedding of St. Catherine (detail).*

The **Cloisters**.   Their entrance is outside the church to the right. The first, though chronologically the last (1537-38), is called St John's or the «door's» («della porta») and features an Ionic colonnade decorated with what remains of late 16th-century frescos. The colonnade's end section connects directly with the next and oldest (1500) or «Chiostro del Capitolo» («Chapterhouse Cloister»), whose wider arcade leads through a superb door, ornately sculpted with aedicules and two-light mullion windows by Antonio Ferrari d'Agrate, to the Chapterhouse. The third or St Benedict's is the largest and dates to 1508-12. Above it is the refectory or dining hall that boasts a Last Supper (1562) by Bedoli with an illusionistic framing fresco attributed to Leonardo da Monchio.

The monastery's first floor is occupied by the **«Biblioteca»** or library. Divided into three aisles by Ionic columns, it is decorated with frescos — a

2

1. *Church of San Giovanni Evangelista. First chapel on the left. Parmigianino. Fresco of the underside of an arch with the saints Lucia and Apollonia. 2. Abbey of San Giovanni Evangelista. Cloister of San Benedetto. 3. Cloister of Capitolo. 4. Spicery room of S. Giovanni Evangelista. Mortar room.*

theatrum mundi and a *theatrum sapientiae* (theatre of the world and of knowledge) — by the Bolognese artists Ercole Pio and Antonio Paganino (1574) that allude to the library's symbolic role as a repository of wisdom. It houses about twenty thousand volumes, including a magnificent collection of illuminated manuscripts.

SPEZIERIA DI SAN GIOVANNI

Literally the «spicery» but actually a pharmacy for the making and dispensing of herbal medicines, it is first mentioned in records dating to 1201, though its being an annex to the monastery would indicate that it is even older and that it probably served the needs of the house long before those of the public.

It owes its present-day appearance to the monastery's rebuilding in the early decades of the 1500s. The pharmacy remained attached to it until 1766, when the Bourbon court's minister of state, Du Tillot, had it secularised and radically altered inside. The vault decorations and the splendid wood-work furnishings date to the late 16th-early 17th century.

THE FIRST ROOM. Called «del Fuoco» or «of the fire» because of the fireplace, it still has its antique counters and 19th-century scales. The walnut shelving, which initially had a clear varnish, contains ceramic and wooden vessels from the 1600s and 1800s. The rather evanescent vault medallion depicting the Assumption is attributed to Innocenzo Martini of Parma (1551-1623).

THE SECOND ROOM. The entry to the «sala dei mortai» or «room of the mortars» has an intaglio eagle, the monastery's symbol, over it. The late-mannerist furnishings contain majolica and ceramic wares from the 17th and 19th centuries as well as marble and bronze mortars of the 17th and 18th centuries. Executed by an anonymous late 16th-century artist, the lunettes' frescos depict the antique world's **Masters of Medicine**, while the central panel portrays the Apparition of the Blessed Trinity to St John.

THE THIRD ROOM. Known as that of the «Sirene» or «of the Sirens» because of the caryatids sculpted into the shelving, which per se is a fine example of mannerist intaglio-work (1606) by Alessandro Vandone and contains valuable editions dating from the 16th through the 19th centuries, it features a painting of the Madonna and Child with Sts John the Evangelist and Benedict dated 1595 (a work of the Venetian school) above the counter and, in the lunettes, early 17th-century portrayals of Parma's illustrious physicians.

By returning to the first room it is possible to visit the laboratory, a small room with its own well, where such items as alembics, bottles and other objects used in preparing medicines can be seen.

SAN FRANCESCO DEL PRATO

The Franciscans came to Parma sometime between 1220-24 and not long thereafter founded their church and monastery of St Francis on the site of what was then known as the «Pratum regium» or royal meadow. This was the area of the fairs and markets; their removal to the «Ghiaia» (gravel) bed on the river left the first official record of the Order of Friars Minor.

The historical records also show that the church's construction was a lengthy affair, finally brought to conclusion in the 15th century. Yet, despite all the halts, the alterations of the monastery in the 1600s and the changes that took place during the Napoleonic era when the building was used as a prison, the church has preserved intact its basic character and much of its original design.

The structure is imposing and Gothic and, unfortunately, in dire need of repair. The façade, crowned by a terracotta frieze featuring a motif of crossed arches and sea shells, is longitudinally divided into three sections by two corner piers and two buttresses marking the interior emphasis. At the centre is the rose window, set off by a brick frame, that was added in 1461 by Alberto da Verona. The main portal is splayed (a

chamfered, sloping surface cut into the walls) and once was adorned by a prothyrum; the right portal is adorned by a dentil-and-foliar terracotta frieze. The walls themselves were compromised by the addition of the numerous open windows that served as light sources for the prison cells.

The interior is divided into a nave and aisles by masonry pillars supporting ogee arches of exceptional span and height on which the trussed roof is sprung. The chapels open off the aisles; those in the left aisle are regular in plan, while those in the right are not uniform. There are two reasons for this: new chapels — St Dorothy's (destroyed in the last century), that of the Conception (now detached from the church) and St Anthony's — were added in the course of time, and because this side was altered to accommodate two floors of prison cells.

1. Ex Church of San Francesco del Prato. Southern side. 2. Front. 3. Oratorio della Concezione.

The polygonal apses are illuminated by ogee-like lancet windows and constitute the only part of the church with ribbed vaulting. The explanation is to be found in the «Narbonais Constitutions» (1260) containing the Franciscan guidelines on church-building that were designed to reconcile the Order's vow of poverty and the appearance of their edifices. In effect they required that only the presbytery area could be emphasized by vaults and that there should be no bell towers — the church's bell tower was a 16th-century addition.

The central apse vault is decorated with frescos by Bartolino de Grossi and Jacopo Loschi, Parma's leading 15th-century artists. In the vault's largest cell or web (compartment) is the figure of Christ the Pantocrator with two virtues on either side; the other cells display a star-spangled sky. The keystone has the sculpted figure of God the Father in the act of benediction, while the walls reveal a female figure of a Franciscan saint beneath which is a painted arch decorated with floral motifs and two tondi or circular pictures enclosing half-busts.

Other frescos have also been found: a portrayal of St Francis receiving the stigmata on the second righthand column, another on the first column left of the presbytery of St Francis, a Crucifix with St John and the pious women on the second lefthand column in the presbytery, a St Nicola da Tolentino (very fragmentary) on the third lefthand column, and a depiction of two saints on the wall between the third and fourth lefthand chapels.

ORATORIO DELLA CONCEZIONE

The Oratory of the Immaculate Conception has a Greek-cross plan with one extended arm that originally linked it to the Church of St Francis. Built between ca. 1521-31, the same period in which the Steccata and the first church of St Rocco were erected, it is one of Parma's most impressive Renaissance examples of a centrally planned building. The design, or rather its attribution, is a matter of some controversy. On the basis of a document of the period (a «pay-to-the-order» note made out to one «Giovan Francesco Pichopietra», with that last word meaning something like «stonecutter»), the art historian and

3

critic A.G. Quintavalle attributes it to G.F. Zaccagni, whereas his colleague, B. Adorni leans towards G.F. d'Agrate.

The frescos decorating the lowered cupola, pendentives and the cross-arm vaults were executed in 1532 by Michelangelo Anselmi and Francesco M. Rondani, collaborators of Correggio. The motifs of the cupola, drum, vaults' coffers and rose windows (these latter with their cherubs and angels) distinctly recall Parmigianino's work in the Steccata.

Particularly noteworthy are the landscape and interior scenes that are part of the pendentives' frescos inspired by the doctrine of the Immaculate Conception. Clearly Mannerist in style, they are depicted in a rather unusual way: as paintings on canvas being held forth to the viewer by youths and maidens.

The altarpiece of the Immaculate Conception (1533-38) by Bedoli is an important work, too. The one on display is a copy of the original now in the National Gallery of Parma.

In 1718 the Oratory was subjected to major alterations. The stucco decorations by Francesco Borra and the ornate illusionistic perspectives by Giovanni Pelliccioli date to this period. The Oratory also has 12 paintings by Clemente Ruta.

TOUR NO. 2

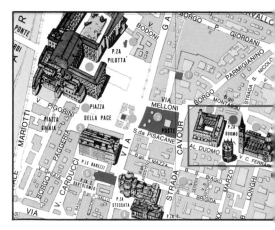

CAMERA DI SAN PAOLO

Originally the private apartment of Giovanna da Piacenza, abbess of the Benedictine Convent of St Paul and today seat of the «Istituto Magistrale», the so-called «Room of St Paul» was superbly frescoed by Correggio (1518-19). The two abbesses immediately preceding her were also from her family and had begun major alterations of both the church and convent. In 1514 Giovanna places the architect Giorgio da Erba in charge of refurbishing the abbess' private apartment. To assure adequate financing of her project, she also transfers the convent's funds to the control of her brother-in-law, Scipione Montino Dalla Rosa. The furor this aroused led to open conflict and culminated in the murder of the previous treasurer in a plot organised by Scipione himself.

The resulting scandal, coupled with the oft-criticised excessive worldliness of monastic life and the open opposition of the civil and religious authorities to the power exercised by the local nobles over the convents and monasteries through the appointment of their younger children to head them, put Giovanna in the eye of the storm. The authorities clamoured for the rein-

statement of the claustral rule, a fixed term for the abbess (then appointed for life) and the enactment of a community property rule.

Giovanna resisted tenaciously, acquiescing to the papal decree only on her deathbed in 1524. With her death, the cloister rule was imposed on the convent and, by force of circumstances, on Correggio's fresco, which remained as secluded as the nuns for two long centuries until being rediscovered by Raffael Mengs while visiting Parma in 1774.

Profane to the exclusion of the sacred, the apartment's fresco derives its exceptional character and interest from the very fact that it was commissioned by an abbess of a convent. Giovanna herself, a learned humanist of undeniable intellectual prowess, Correggio and perhaps a scholar friend or two of the abbess planned the work in detail. It denotes a thorough knowledge of mythology and preference for its more erudite and unusual themes. Some of the allusions are so recondite in fact that only those who were initiated to their secret mysteries could decipher the references to the abbess' personal struggle to assert her intellectual and social independence in the face of interference from bishops and the pope.

The **room** itself is almost square, and Correggio has transformed the spatial arrangement of the umbrella vault into a «berceau» or bamboo cradle with a luxuriant climber. The vault's keystone bears the sculpted coat of arms of the abbess — three crescent moons entwined with pink ribbons supporting clusters of hanging fruit. The sixteen ribs radiating from the keystone are painted to simulate bamboo and give rise to just as

---

1. View of Via M. Melloni and the ex-Palazzo di Riserva; on the right-hand there's the entrance to Camera di S. Paolo. (St Paul's room). 2. Camera di San Paolo. Correggio. The vault

many concave lozenges with ovolo moulding in which are depicted putti playing with hunting arms, dogs and so on, against a background of sky. The ribs spring from false capitals decorated with rams' heads; from one to the next head are taut tablecloths bearing plates, ewers and crockery alluding to the room's function as dining hall.

The critical interpretation of the Camera has a rather complex history. Many and divergent have been the views expressed by the scholars who have contributed to the substantial literature on the subject. The fresco cycle has been explained, for example, as an allegory of life (Barilli, 1906), as symbolic of hunting (Ricci, 1930), and from a strictly formal standpoint (Longhi, 1956). The version that follows is a synopsis of Panovsky's iconographic analysis (1961).

The noble-born Giovanna peeks from the hearth in the robes of Diana the moon goddess — an obvious reference to the moons in her coat of arms. Like the haughty goddess, she too appears ready to pit her tenacity against opponents and detractors.

Iconographically speaking, the fresco is to be viewed beginning with the lunettes on the west wall, which originally was the first to greet the visitor entering the room (the present-day entrance is a later addition). Here is Pan, half-human half-goat, blowing into a conch to instill «panic and terror» into the heart of the young maiden intrepidly approaching him with a dove, symbol of innocence and sincerity. She is a portrait of Giovanna, who stood her ground undaunted by the clamour of those who would deny her freedom.

She is followed by another maiden bearing a lily, symbol of virginity and chastity, while the scene is a metaphor of the nuns that remained faithful to Giovanna in her struggle against her adversaries. It also symbolises their victory over those who tried to ensnare them in a tangle of harsh rules.

The ovolo mouldings with putti, which at cursory glance might seem to refer to Diana as huntress, rather reinforce and complete the meaning of the lunette scenes. So, for instance, one of the putti in the oval above Pan succeeds where the god fails — by blowing into his horn he deafens his companion and forces him to cover his ears.

The narrative thread continues on the north wall. Here two antithetical forces are face to face: Bellona, goddess of war and destruction, brandishing a torch and the Three Graces, Amity, Harmony and Peace, dancing. Over the hearth, beneath the two lunettes, is the motto «ignem gladio ne fodias» (you will not arouse the fire with the sword). This is Giovanna's sarcastic challenge to her zealous enemies that they not use force to achieve what they cannot obtain.

At the far left is a maiden holding a cornucopia in one hand and a helm resting on a globe in the other — Fortune (Fortuna Augusti). At the far right a naked youth with garlanded head and spear in hand represents virtue. Fortune and Virtue confront one another as ever conflicting life forces.

To the south we find the three Fates busy at their work: Clotho holding the distaf or spool about which the thread of life is spun, Lachesis unravelling it and Atropos cutting it with scissors — admonitory personifications of that destiny which no one can escape. The contrast between Lachesis lengthening life and Atropos cutting it short is further underscored by the leafy tree behind the former and the bare branches behind the latter. This idea is further strengthened by the objects below the three figures: a laurel branch lies by Clotho and an axe by Atropos, symbol of death.

To the left is depicted the temple of Capitoline Jove followed by a bearded old man with a spike of wheat in his hand: Melancholy personified as Saturn, who dethroned his father, Uranus, and then devoured all his children but Jove, who was saved by his mother's stratagem and, upon reaching adulthood, then usurped his father's throne and condemned him to the darkness of Tartarus.

The fourth lunette depicts a woman bearing a child to safety: the child Jupiter (Jove), whose temple is shown on the left, saved from the devouring father, Sa-

turn. The goddess depicted in the next lunette on the west wall appears to be welcoming him in offering Jupiter the globe, symbol of dominion over the world. She is probably Diana Lucifer, the goddess who brings light to the newborn by helping them come forth from the darkness of the maternal womb. Briefly put, these scenes bring home to the viewer that no one can escape their destiny, that which has been preordained; not even Jupiter who, like Saturn before him, is also subject to the Fates.

The east wall portrays the four elements as personified by Tellus as earth (second lunette on the left), Juno as air, suffering the punishment described by Homer (suspended in mid-air with two golden anvils under her feet), Vesta as fire on the right (here is the task of keeping the eternal flame lit), and Genius as water (a divinity associated with well-being).

This was the wall through which one originally entered the room and, by so doing, began a journey through the four elements — an act that has been likened to a purifying bath elevating the spirit (the mirror of nature). Indeed, the inscription on one of the fireplaces reads «we passed through fire and water».

The north wall portrays the figures of peace and war, fortune and virtue — the powers governing human existence. Opposite, on the west wall, purity triumphs over Pan, showing the viewer the path to follow (the moral mirror), while on the south wall we are reminded that we cannot elude our destiny (the mirror of doctrine).

The room's erudite decoration bespeaks the learned pantheistic spirit of the abbess, whereas the inspiration for the monochrome figures of the classical gods is mainly drawn from ancient Roman coins of which many humanists in northern Italy were collectors.

Some scholars have put forth the theory that Correggio had been to Rome before executing these frescos. This would explain his supposed knowledge of such important contemporary works as Raphael's Segnatura room, the Chigi Chapel in S. Maria del Popolo and Mantegna's Vittoria della Madonna (he had been Mantegna's pupil), for the idea of the bamboo bower motif, all in Rome.

---

1. Camera di S. Paolo. Detail of the vault. 2. Detail of the vault. 3. Detail of a monochromatic lunette.

Hours: Tues-Sat 9am-2pm, Sundays & Holidays 9am-1pm. Closed Mondays.

CAMERA DELL'ARALDI. This room, which had originally been a part of Giovanna da Piacenza's private apartment, was frescoed in 1514 by Alessandro Araldi, as can be seen on the fireplace inscription. The intellectual distance that separates the two artists is immediately evident. Unlike Correggio, who is thoroughly imbued with Renaissance culture, Araldi is still bridled by late Gothic conceptions, despite efforts to achieve a modern style that can be noted in the grotesque decorations.

Against the blue background of the vault that features an illusionistic oculus (circular opening) at its centre about which are putti, he has portrayed a com-

plex group of fabulous beings framing scenes in panels of the Old and New Testaments. The lunettes contain allegorical and mythological compositions: the story of the nereid Cydippe (back wall); the Impossible, two feet walking on water (left); Ceres; Divine Love; a priestess in nun's habit; two Virtues pitted against a dragon and monkey; and the Roman Charity, a triumph, and the virgin and unicorn.

1. Camera dell'Araldi. The vault. 2. Piazzale della Pace. The ex-Palazzo di Riserva with the entrance to Glauco Lombardi Museum.

MUSEO GLAUCO LOMBARDI

The Museum is housed in rooms belonging to the large 17th-century building that was once property of the dukes and is bounded by Via Cavour, Via Melloni, Piazzale della Pace and Via Pisacane. Its interior halls and rooms have included in the past the ducal theatre, designed by Stefano Lolli in 1687 and torn down with the building of the new Teatro Regio, several court apartments and the foresteria or quarters reserved for important guests of the duke. This latter function was also the source of its name, **Palazzo di Riserva** («reserve palace»). The part that the Museum Lombardi occupies had even been remodelled in 1764 by the ducal architect E.A. Petitot as a Casino for nobles and courtiers.

The museum's entrance is through a door of the neoclassical façade that gives on to Piazzale della Pace.

Inaugurated in 1961, the museum is the result of the labours and devotion of Prof. Glauco Lombardi. His unflagging enthusiasm and tenacity enabled him to recover the art works, household objects and furnishings from court residences that otherwise would have found their way to antiques dealers. The museum is the end result.

The collections are interesting not only *per se* as art but also for their value as a record of the life and customs of court history spanning more than a century (mid-18th to mid-19th centuries). Its focal point is the figure of Marie Louise, Napoleon's wife and Duchess of Parma, Piacenza and Guastalla from 1816 to 1847. She was beloved by her subjects and still remembered today. The items in the museum's possession reconstruct her public image and private life.

The «Grande Salone». The ornate ceiling stuccos were designed by Petitot and executed by Benigno Bossi. The «grand salon» displays include: an elegant formal gown and mantle worn by the duchess for official ceremonies, the nuptial «corbeille» in the centre, which was designed by Pierre-Paul Prud'Hon and given to her by Napoleon as a wedding gift (1810), and, on the back wall, the portrait of Marie Louise, Empress of France, painted in 1812 by Robert Lefevre. To one side of the canvas is a charcoal and watercolour portrait of Napoleon by F. Gerard and, to the other, a portrait by Prud'Hon of Marie Louise and Napoleon's son (King of Rome and Duke of Reistach) in the guise of Love asleep. Copies of this work are known to exist.

Other portraits adorn the walls, and the display cases contain jewellery and personal objects belonging to the Duchess, Napoleon and their son.

The Sala Dorata. Other objects of Marie Louise are on display here in the «Gold Room». Noteworthy are: the «Coppa della Puerpera» by P.L. Dagoty; an oil sketch of the Teatro Regio's curtain by Giovan Battista Borghesi (on the right as you enter); and the historically interesting watercolours by G. Naudin on the walls that are faithful recreations of the now demolished Palazzo Ducale's interior rooms.

The next room. This is dedicated to the engravings of **PAOLO TOSCHI**, director of the Academy of Fine Arts and founder of an important school for engraving. In the centre is a silk-embroidered mantle given to Marie Louise by the Chinese Emperor Kia King Kan.

The walls boast a fine display of 19th-century painting at Parma.

THE SALA DEGLI ACQUARELLI. The «room of the watercolours» contains engravings, paintings and watercolours of the 18th and 19th centuries executed by artists from Parma, Italy and foreign countries.

THE SALA DEI FRANCESI. The «French room» boasts Marie Louise's piano in the centre, on which is the score of I Lombardi alla Prima Crociata («The Lombards on the First Crusade») that Verdi dedicated to Marie Louise. The display cases contain personal objects of the Duchess, including a portable writing desk and bronze and terracotta sculptures. French, Italian and local paintings adorn the walls.

THE SIXTH ROOM. This is dedicated to the architect **PETITOT**. The collection includes an interesting series of drawings, engravings, sketches and plans of both completed and proposed projects.

THE MARIE LOUISE ROOM. The last, it contains more personal effects of the Duchess, including an embroidery case, fishing tackle and artist's case. At the back of the room to the right is a small marble bust made from a model by Lorenzo Bartolini of Count Adam Neipperg, morganatic husband of Marie Louise, whom she wed in 1821.

Hours: Tues-Sat 9am-2pm, Sundays & Holidays 9am-1pm. Closed Mondays.

---

1. Museo Glauco Lombardi. The Grande Salone: on foreground a sumptuous dress of the Duchess Maria Luigia, whose portrait, by R. Lefevre, is on the background; in the middle of the room there's the wedding corbeille that was given her as a present by Napoleon. 2. The Golden room that shows the precious Coppa della Puerpera by P.L. Dagoty.

TEATRO REGIO

Occupying the site of the medieval Benedictine monastery of St Alexander, the theatre was commissioned by Marie Louise to replace that in Palazzo di Riserva, one of the several Farnese theatres, which had outlived its usefulness.

Built between 1821 and 1829, the imposing new edifice is an example of the architectural tradition in theatre design that produced such gems as Milan's La Scala, Venice's La Fenice and Naples' San Carlo. As elsewhere, the theatre in Parma was now open to the public, a fact which made it, like the Palazzo Ducale, a focal point in the city's urban fabric and its cultural life. The new features included foyer, tiered boxes, rooms be-

hind the boxes, box-office, cloakroom and caffè, all conceived to accommodate large audiences. The theatre had become a social service, even a social event for the upper bourgeoisie, as well as the sacred temple of the operatic melodrama, which at Parma means Verdi first and foremost, by long-standing tradition and a public that is famous for its passionate involvement and expertise.

The Teatro (the appellative «Regio» or royal dates to 1849) was designed by the ducal architect Nicola Bettoli, the chief exponent of the Neoclassical at Parma. The façade is moved by a portico supported by ten

Ionic columns and surmounted by two tiered strips. The second of these features a large arched window flanked on either side by bas-reliefs of Fame, the work of the sculptor Tommaso Bandini. He also did the relief of the lyre and classical masks at the centre of the tympanum.

Under the portico are the three entrances that lead to the box-office and atrium, with the latter's two rows of Ionic columns and fine lacunar ceiling. Off the atrium are the caffè, cloakroom, smoking room and (west side) the entrance to the auditorium.

The traditional horseshoe-plan is accented by tiered rows of boxes surmounted by the gallery. The ornate royal box is in the centre, directly opposite the stage.

The gilt and white stucco decorations are by Gerolamo Magnani, who replaced the original «chiaroscuro» ones when the theatre was restored in 1853. The decorations of the proscenium boxes flanking the stage are even more ornate. They are framed by a rich frieze bearing medallions with busts of poets and opera composers (Bellini, Donizetti, Torelli, and so forth). Four large corbels support the coffered stage arch the frontispiece of which features an illuminated clock.

The ceiling boasts a «grand» chandelier by Auguste Lacerriere of Paris and portraits of the great playwrights: Linus, Aristophanes, Euripides, Plautus, Seneca, Metastasio, Alfieri and Goldoni by Giovan Battista Borghesi, who also painted the **curtain** depicting the «Triumph of Minerva», goddess of Wisdom.

The marble staircase in the atrium leads up to the «ridotto» or foyer above the auditorium's entrances. It is actually a series of rooms, including a large rectangular salon decorated by local artists in the early 19th century.

The Teatro Regio was inaugurated on 16th May 1829 with the premiere of Zaira, which Vincenzo Bellini composed for the occasion. It was not, by the way, received well by the audience.

1. The Teatro Regio. External view. 2. Teatro Regio. G.B. Borghesi. The Sipario with the representation of the Trionfo di Minerva.

'ANTA MARIA DELLA STECCATA

More familiarly known simply as the «Stecca-
a», from the word for fence, it was originally a
mall oratorio containing a Madonna that was
eld in particular veneration by the populace. In
521, in thanksgiving to the Virgin for a victory
ver French troops on 21st December, the comune allotted a healthy sum for the construction
f a church. It became a symbol of the city's col-
ctive faith, and as such, so we find in the chroni-
les of the day, everyone contributed according
o his means either money or labour to the build-
g (completed in 1539).

It is one of the finest examples of early 16th-
entury centrally planned churches, and its de-
gn reveals traces of the humanist ideal ex-
ounded by Leon Battista Alberti that aspired to
e erection of a «perfect temple». Its distinct
enaissance conception is also the source of the
roblem involved in attribution.

It is known with certainty that the actual build-
rs were Bernardino Zaccagni and his son, Gio-
an Francesco, whose work on other buildings in
arma suggest that they were still linked to cer-
in medieval concepts. This contrasts with very
recise typological affinities that the church's de-

sign shares with drawings of Leonardo, who at
the time had contacts on several occasions with
Parma.

The traditional attribution of Bramante is
from Vasari, but this appears unlikely as the former's collaborator, Antonio da Sangallo the
younger, makes no mention of him when called
upon in 1526 for advice on the church's building.
Having come to Parma to examine its defensive
works, Sangallo supplied the cupola's design,
which bears strong resemblance to that of St Peter's in Rome.

The Zaccagnis also ran into problems. There
were conflicts with those who had commissioned
the work, and, after being subjected to review by
special commissions (on which Correggio even
sat), they were dismissed in 1525. The building
was finished by Giovan Francesco d'Agrate,
who also did the ornamental marbles, and Marcantonio Zucchi.

The crowning balustrade, adorned with statues, vases and festoons, is Baroque and was
added by Mauro Oddi in 1696. In 1725, when
the church had become the seat of the Constantinian Order of the Knights of St George, d'Agrate's original sacristy was demolished to make
room for the Knight's choir, designed by the ar-

chitect Adalberto Della Nave of Parma. This new addition is marked by a local taste for the scenographic; it is noticeably anti-classical in style and highly emphasised. An interesting detail is to be seen in the outside cornice that has been extended to cover the mixed-line profiles of the windows.

The interior. Of Greek-cross plan, it features chapels in the four corner towers and richly decorative vault frescos.

The presbytery arch. Begun in 1530 and finished in 1539, the decoration is one of Parmigianino's masterpieces. The red background of the arch is divided into coffers, each bearing intricately rendered floral motifs in gilded copper. Three virgins at the end points stand with vases containing lilies on their heads and lamps in their hands (with flame in the left and without in the right). The entire motif is outlined by two blue bands bearing the monochrome figures of Adam, Eve, Aaron and Moses flanking the canephorae (female figures with baskets, i.e. vases in this case, on their heads).

The festoon-like floral motifs of the coffers represent allegories of the four elements: fruit and flowers spring from the earth and, like the rams' heads, are i

1. Church of S. Maria della Steccata. 2. The banisters of M Oddi and the dome designed by Antonio da Sangallo il Gio vane. 3. The interior.

ymbols; the sea shells and crabs symbolise water; the
oves air; and the brilliant gold colour of the coffering
re. This is a favourite theme of Renaissance culture
– the microcosm is the emblematic reflection of the
nacrocosm.

The virgins have been interpreted in various ways
y critics. Their distinguishing feature is the presence
r absence of the lamp flame, whence the connexion
to the parable of the Ten Virgins, with its allusion to
he fall from grace and exclusion from the joys of para-
ise. There also seems to be a reference in the portray-
l of the central virgin's handing the lamps to the other
wo to the Church (the wise virgin) and the Synagogue
the foolish virgin), i.e. their respective ability and in-
bility to impart light (divine grace). So, too, the wise
irgins undoubtedly symbolise the Virgin Mary as
Virgo prudentissima». The friezes beneath the arch,
epicting books and other liturgical objects, complete
he decoration.

The decoration itself is tempera on the wall and was
xecuted with the aid of a cartoon (detailed drawing
n paper) and the help of others to fix it. The sinuous
ines of the tapering figures and the restless rustle of
heir robes are examples of Parmigianino's mature
Mannerism, just as the iconographic complexities il-
ustrate the hermetic content of his art. This compo-
ent also comes to the fore in Vasari's description of
he artist as a most handsome youth whose passion for
lchemy transformed him into a «wild man». Whether
ecause of this, or because of the many years it took to
omplete the work, Parmigianino ran very much afoul
f those who were in charge of the building. These al-
ercations brought about his arrest, followed by his es-
ape to Casalmaggiore where he died shortly after-
vards at the age of 37 — probably, as Vasari mentions,
oisoned by the harmful vapours from his alchemical
xperiments.

The apse vault is decorated with a portrayal of Our
Lady Queen of Heaven. Originally one of Parmigiani-
o's commissions, it was executed from 1540 to 1547
y Michelangelo Anselmi working from the cartoons
f Giulio Romano. The rendering reveals a certain un-
veness ascribable to the different styles of the two
rtists, a fact which also made the transfer from car-
oon to wall problematic. The Siena mannerist Ansel-
ni emphasises the restless line and «chiaroscuro» ef-
ects (light-shadow balance) while Romano is more
he monumentalist.

Anselmi also did the arch and the Adoration of the
Magi fresco (1548-59) in the large west niche (the later was finished by Bernardino Gatti because of Anselmi's untimely death).

Girolamo Mazzola Bedoli executed the decora-
ions (ca. 1547-67) depicting the Pentecost and Na-
ivity on the north and south vaults, respectively, and
he remaining two large arches that follow Parmigiani-
o's lead. A second-generation mannerist who was
strongly influenced by Parmigianino, Bedoli mani-
ests a pronounced penchant for the virtuoso display
n his vault compositions, a marked contrast to his
work on the arches. There, while following the concept of his predecessor (Parmigianino), his composi-
ion is quite personal and intimate, effects he achieved
through the use of delicate colours and their gradual
onal transitions that are clearly distinct from the line-
arity of Parmigianino.

The cupola. The fresco of the Assumption is the
work of Bernardo Gatti (nicknamed «Sojaro»), who
executed it from 1560 to 1570. The fresco faces south,
where the main entrance was before being closed off
in 1762. Although the figures are somewhat academic
in their reference to Michelangelo, the work as a
whole is clearly inspired by Correggio's cupola in the
Duomo. It should be noted, too, that Sojaro has employed a far less dramatic illusionism for the sky, eli-
minated Correggio's «dangling legs» and portrayed

3

his figures in a more rigid and traditional manner than Correggio — he may have had in mind the polemics that so discouraged his illustrious predecessor.

The high altar fresco of the Virgin nursing the infant Jesus, executed by a local artist in the late 15th century, is the devotional image for which the church was named.

On the wall to the right of the church's entrance are two paintings for organ doors by Parmigianino. They portray David and St Cecilia; the Flemish artist J. Sons retouched them and added something of his own at a later date. Sons also executed the other two organ-door paintings (to the left of the presbytery) depicting the Flight into Egypt (late 16th century); they gave him an opportunity to display his skill as a landscapist.

The inside front wall has an Annunciation by the Cremonese painter Malosso (Giovan Battista Trotti),

. Church of S. Maria della Steccata. Parmigianino. Arch with the wise Virgins and the foolish Virgins. 2. Detail of the arch: ne of the foolish Virgins. 3. Detail of the arch. 4. Detail of the ieze.

dating to the late 16th century. In the niche to the right is a St George Slaying the Dragon (1718). rendered in a coldly academic classicism by Marc'Antonio Franceschini. The niche on the left boasts the «pala» or altarpiece of the Holy Trinity and Saints, with its evident Bolognese classicism, by G. Battista Cignaroli (1764).

Noteworthy, too, are the funerary monuments, especially that of Count Adam Neipperg, Marie Louise's morganatic husband, which was executed in the neoclassical style by Lorenzo Bartolini in 1829-31.

The «**Sacrestia Nobile**». The splendid wood furnishings of the sacristy are the work (1665) of G. Battista Mascheroni and Carlo Rottini, both of Milan, and Rinaldo Torra of Parma. The compositional exuberance is a hallmark of the Baroque. The sacristy also has a collection of valuable vestments of the 16th,

17th and 18th centuries, and its altarpiece of the Holy Family (1607) is by J. Sons.

Downstairs, Marie Louise had a sepulchral chapel built to house the tombs of the Farnese and Bourbon dukes.

In the small square outside the church is the marble **Monument to Parmigianino**, sculpted in 1879 by Giovanni Chierici to honour the artist who dedicated his finest and most emblematic works to the «Steccata». The crests of the City of Parma and the Constantinian Order, which promoted and financed the statue, appear on the pedestal.

SANT'ALESSANDRO

Originally a Benedictine convent and church erected in the 9th century and demolished in 1821 to make room for the Teatro Regio, St Alexander's church is all that remains today. It was rebuilt in the early 16th century by the architect Bernardino Zaccagni of Parma and further altered in 1622 by the architect Giovan Battista Magnani, who had been commissioned by the abbess Maura Lucenia, whose real name was Margherita Farnese, daughter of Duke Alessandro.

The neoclassical façade was added in 1784 and is the work of Antonio Bettoli. The interior is a harmonious and balanced display of architecture and decoration that was common of a style practised in this part of Italy (the Emilia) by Vigarani (1588-1663) and the Bibienas.

The aisless nave features two chapels per side that are framed by serlianas (or serlian motif), which also are repeated at the entry to the chancel area and on the inside façade wall (painted).

Magnani also executed St Alexander's urn on the high altar, where it is framed by softly draping polychrome marble. The altarpiece of the Virgin and Child with Sts Justine, Benedict and Alexander is by Girolamo Mazzola Bedoli (ca. 1540).

The nave vaults are decorated with ornate illusionistic balconies adorned with putti and angelic musicians by the quadraturista of the Bolognese school Michele Colonna (1625).

The cupola decoration, in which the influence of Correggio can also be seen in the clear, delicate colours, was executed in 1627 by Alessandro Tiarini. It depicts Christ and a genuflecting Magdalen encircled by saints, angels and putti. Tiarini also did the wall painting of the martyrdom of St Alexander (pope) to the right of the presbytery.

1. Church of S. Alessandro. The interior. 2. The weekly market in the square behind the Church of S. Bartolomeo. 3. The courtyard called della Pilotta, formerly S. Pietro Martire, one of the great open spaces of the Farnese building.

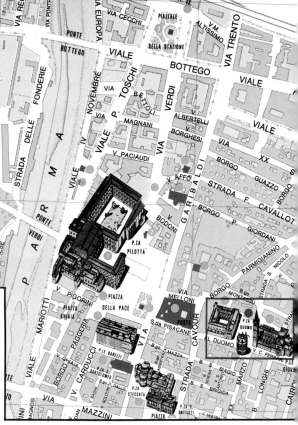

TOUR NO. 3

dences. It occupied an area that once linked the court palaces located between today's Via Cavour and Piazzale della Pace and the palazzo of government and the summer residence. These latter were situated in the «cross-river» area and were reached by the wooden Galleria bridge that was reserved for the use of the Farneses. In the

THE PILOTTA

Built around three inner quadrangles, the imposing complex of palazzi was the idea of Duke Ranuccio I Farnese. The Pilotta was designed to house court services: storehouses, stables, hay lofts, the secret archives, treasury and a grandiose arms magazine that was later transformed into a theatre. The site it occupies was already a partially developed area when the complex was begun, so that the vast proportions of the Pilotta made it a symbol of Farnese power. The name itself derives from a corruption of the term for the game «pelota», which was played along with what was then called «raquette» ball by the nobility in the courtyards of their palazzi.

The complex was conceived as a structure that would integrate the intricate system of ducal resi-

3

73

end it gave rise to a city-within-the-city, secluded and detached from the court proper.

Even before Ranuccio, his father Ottavio had a covered passageway called the «corridore» or corridor built to connect these same two sites. Almost certainly designed by the architect Francesco Paciotto of Urbino, the corridor was later incorporated into the first two storeys of the Pilotta's south building, the one that faces the «Ghiaia», with its courtyard open to automobile traffic. With its massive arcade and stylized, horizontal and vertical strips as decorative motif emphasising a double gallery and the mezzanine's smaller one, Paciotto's austere structure served as a model and point of departure for Ranuccio, who had its modular form repeated in his grandiose project.

1. La Pilotta. 2. The imperial main staircase of S. Moschino with octagonal dome. 3. The group of building of La Pilotta seen from the Oltretorrente.

Work began in 1602, and the duke was undoubtedly a direct participant right from the outset. This was perfectly in character and keeping with the Farneses and their tradition of being meticulous planners in matters of building and ornament. Likelihood would assign the task of proceeding where Paciotto had left off to Simone Moschino of Orvieto, who was then the court's chief engineer and in charge of several other important city projects.

The first of the quadrangles to be completed was that over the corridor. This is the one that is today called Pilotta but was then known as St Peter Martyr's, for it incorporated the Dominican convent of the same name that had been wedged into the quadrangle at the north-east corner of the side that now faces Via Garibaldi. This religious house was razed during the Napoleonic ban on certain institutions (something which the Farneses were never able to achieve), and the gaping wound that was left can still be seen.

The remaining two quadrangles are the «Guazzatoio», so named because, as the largest, the horses were watered there, and the «Rochetta» to the south-west. Its name means «small rock» but was synonymous with the term for fort; in this case the Visconti one which it incorpor-

ated as can be seen from traces of that original edifice in the side facing the river.

Work was halted in 1611. The façade on the «Ghiaia» side was never completed, despite three distinct designs in as many periods: originally by Moschino, later by Pier Francesco Battistelli of Bologna (at Parma from 1510 to 1524) and finally by Geronimo Rainaldi of Rome (1570-1655).

Almost certainly by Moschino and, hence, part of the original building is the grand «imperial» stairway leading to the original military training hall. It has a peculiar form: an initial flight leading to the landing with two other flights branching off from and parallel to it. The rather imposing form strongly suggests the stairway of the Escorial at Madrid as model; it may even have been the duke himself who proposed it. The rectangle comprising the two upper flights is covered by a large ribbed octagonal cupola. Apart from the already mentioned transformation of its magazine into a theatre in 1618, the Pilotta has not undergone radical alterations of a structural nature since work was halted.

When the Bourbons succeeded the Farneses, they changed its function not its foundations. They refurbished certain rooms to accommod-

ate the Museum of Antiquities, the Palatine Library, the Art Gallery (Pinacoteca) and the Academy in the Palazzo of the Cultural Institutions where they are still housed today.

This basically is the Pilotta we see today: the unfinished façade and the unresolved problem of the convent that broke the symmetry of the first quadrangle. Its imposing mass is even more out of scale with the rest of the cityscape today than before. This is the result of the razing of the court residences that stood behind it during the rule of the Bourbon dukes. This is a far cry from the idea, and Petitot's project, at the time to build a more dignified Palazzo Ducale — a plan that was never brought to fruition. The gaping aperture on the Via Garibaldi side was partially remedied by Marie Louise, who had Bettoli erect a proper façade on what remained of the court residences (altogether destroyed during the Second World War).

A definitive arrangement of this large area that is presently a car-park is now under study. It will, however, not be an easy task to reconcile with the cityscape a complex that stands as a veritable antithesis to it, especially since this part of the Pilotta has been reduced to an appendage of the city's traffic grid.

MONUMENTO A VERDI

Facing the buttresses of the Pilotta is the *«ara»* or memorial altar dedicated to Giuseppe Verdi (1813-1901), made of granite from the San Fidelino quarries with bronzes in relief by Ettore Ximenes. Seated in a pose of pensive reflection, the figure of the «maestro» stands out among the front high-relief sculptures depicting in elegant and sinuous lines male and female figures representing the allegories Inspiration, Melody, Simphony, Song, Hate and Love, Sacred Song, the Dance, the Betrayed and Love.

On the back are three bas-relief panels portraying important historical events representing Verdi's patriotism. Centre: A crowd holding aloft signs with the famous Risorgimento slogan "Viva Verdi". Left: Scene depicting the annexation of Parma to the constitutional Kingdom of Savoy (1859). Right: The commemoration of this event as symbolised by Verdi shaking hands with King Victor Emanuel II.

As seen today, the memorial no longer occupies its original site, which was part of the far more imposing tribute that the city dedicated to the maestro on the hundredth anniversary of his

birth, a centenary monument that reflected the commemorative architectural idiom then current in Italy. Begun in 1913 by the architect Lamberto Cusani, the memorial was a stately arcaded exedra with the altar at the centre and occupied the site of the current Enel building that stands before the station and that already boasted the monument to Bottego. Despite the inevitable polemics, the enclosure was demolished after the war, victim of the building boom, and the altar itself was transferred to its present site in 1947.

1. Pilotta Square. The altar of the Monument of G. Verdi. 2. Detail of the altorilievo of the altar with the Maestro surrounded by allegoric figures. 3. Detail of the altorilievo of the altar. The Maestro.

3

MUSEO ARCHEOLOGICO NAZIONALE

The inception of a Museum of Antiquities was part of Du Tillot's enlightened policies under the aegis of Philip of Bourbon. Its *raison d'être* was the discovery of the Roman town at Veleia in 1747.

The artifacts were originally housed in the Galleria of the Biblioteca Farnese («Gallery of the Farnese Library») and in the Academy. This practise was begun in 1760 under the curatorship of Antonio Costa. He was succeeded by Paolo M. Paciaudi, who in turn was followed by Pietro de Lama in 1799, the prime mover behind the idea of the Museum.

The collection itself soon included works of ancient art from the Farnese collection, artifacts from the excavations at Luceria (Reggio Emilia) in 1776-86 and valuable numismatic collections acquired through the years. During the era of Marie Louise and the curatorship of De Lama, the Museum again adds to its collections. Beginning in 1816, it acquires the inscriptions from the church of St Augustine at Piacenza and, in 1831, a veritable treasure of coins and jewellery from excavations at the site of the Teatro Regio, then under construction.

From 1825 to 1867, under the curatorship of Michele Lopez, the Museum's collections continued to grow with the addition of coins, Greek vases and Egyptian artifacts. These latter objects were the fruit of studies in Egyptology, which had come to prominence at the time (1830-32). In 1841-42, during excavations of the road bed in Via Farini, remains of the Roman theatre were discovered, part of which went to the Museum. The Academy gave the Museum its twelve statues from the Veleia basilica in 1866.

The prehistoric collection was the idea of Luigi Pigorini, curator of the Museum from 1867 to 1875. The heterogeneous nature of these collections was typical of 19th-century Museums in general.

A more orderly and logical arrangement of the material was first undertaken by G. Monaco (1933-58). His work has been continued, under current museographical criteria, by Mansuelli who has separated the archaeological from the Medieval art collections (with the latter now under the curatorship of the proper government agency).

The FIRST ROOM: Some of the sculptures here are from the Gonzaga Collection of Guastalla.

SECOND ROOM: It houses the Egyptian collection (begun about 1830), which includes amulets, necklaces, figurines, funerary scarabs, sarcophagi, canopic vases, and the like.

THIRD ROOM: Sculptures from the Gonzaga and Farnese collections.

FOURTH ROOM: Numismatic collection, begun during Bourbon rule, with later additions, featuring about 20,000 coins of Greek, Roman, Italian, Medieval and modern origins.

FIFTH ROOM: The 19th-century vault fresco is by F Scaramuzza. On display are twelve statues of members of the Julius Claudia family unearthed at Veleia

SIXTH ROOM: Featured is the «Tabula Alimentaria Veleiate», discovered in 1747. It records the provisions of the «istitutio alimentaria» (a sort of food procurement act) by Nerva and Trajan concerning Veleia and the surrounding area.

Also on display is the bronze tablet of the *«Lex de Gallia Cisalpina»* (Law of Cisalpine Gaul) dating to the Roman Republic. Among the small bronzes in the display cases is the *«Drunken Hercules»* (all are from Veleia).

SEVENTH ROOM: Etruscan artifacts from the Hellenistic age, including funerary urns and Hellenistic and Attic ceramics.

In the corridor leading to the ground floor is the epigraphic collection (inscriptions).

GROUND FLOOR, FIRST ROOM on the left: Paleolithic Neolithic and Bronze Age artifacts. SECOND ROOM. Terremare culture artifacts from Castione Marchesi

LUIGI PIGORINI ROOM (third): The Bronze Age objects in the display cases were found at Parma and surrounding areas.

FIRST ROOM (right of atrium): Roman artifacts from settlements in the Parma countryside. SECOND ROOM Roman inscriptions, bronzes from the Roman theatre in the displays and a circular funerary monument. Also included are mile-stones from the late-empire period and archaeological artifacts from city excavations.

Hours: Tues-Sat 9am-2pm, Sundays & Holidays 9am-1pm. Closed Mondays.

1

1. Museo Archeologico Nazionale. The 5ᵗʰ Room with the 12 statues representing members of Giulio-Claudia family. 2. Teatro Farnese. The cavea.

TEATRO FARNESE

The theatre's entrance, on the first floor of the Palazzo della Pilotta, is marked by a wooden door painted to simulate marble and crowned by an imposing pediment bearing the Farnese coat of arms. It was built in 1618 under Ranuccio I and skillfully restored following its more or less complete destruction by a bomb during World War II.

The Farnese is a theatre in the Renaissance court tradition of the term — secluded, private, for the exclusive enjoyment of the prince and his guests. These theatres were generally situated in rooms set aside for the purpose in the palazzi of the aristocracy and made do with rather makeshift structures.

This theatre, however, was a bit the exception to the rule — it was housed in the vast hall that Ranuccio had recently had built for training at arms. It went beyond the princely prototype of the court theatre, or better, it carried that concept to its extreme: it was a precursor of the large public theatre. Therein lies its unique historical importance.

The Farnese stage was different from the Renaissance concept in another important aspect.

Although built entirely of wood, its machinery was no longer makeshift. Its dimensions, capacity and its imposing architectonic structures make it a permanent focal point of the building that houses it.

The impression it must have imparted at the time can only be imagined: the original, ornate decorations — the restoration was only able to refurbish the wood panelling — creating a brilliant and glittering illusion of splendour.

All the architectural elements were painted to simulate marble and adorned with stucco statues in imitation of Carrara marble: Apollo and the Muses with other divinities along the upper balustrade, allegories in the proscenium niches, and torch-bearing putti along the lower balustrade.

A vaulted ceiling covered the auditorium with its illusionistic decorations depicting two loggias crowded with spectators, as if in continuation of the real audience, and Jupiter in glory at the centre. The entire room was illuminated by four immense chandeliers, each one having 300 tapers.

Grandiose and imposing of form and space, in which reality and illusion mingled in the life and mind of the spectator. The particular circumstance that caused the theatre to be built in the first place is as intriguing as the room itself. It was

1

hurried from conception to completion by the news that Cosimo II dei Medici would visit Parma. The Farnese court spared no effort to impress their guest, for the family wished to arrange the marriage of prince Odoardo and Cosimo's daughter, Margherita.

The Medicis were to be courted by the Farneses in the grand style. The theatre was to be the focal point of that magnificence, the keystone of the festivities. In short, it became an instrument of court politics. At Parma more than elsewhere, the theatre was used to display princely pageants, to unite amusement and marvelling wonder in the pursuit of policy. The theatre was the stage from which the Farnese court celebrated itself and impressed its guests.

The theatre had therefore to be designed so as to astound even the jaded sensibilities of the duke. The task fell to one «Argenta» (Giovan Battista Aleotti of Ferrara), architect of civil and religious buildings but, above all, famed for his theatre designs and scene settings of extraordinary imagination.

In little over a year (late 1617-1618) he built an entire theatre of fir wood furnishings that encompassed three distinct areas: tiered rows of seats surmounted by loggias, the stage and, linking these two areas, two lateral triumphal arches with their stucco equestrian statues of Ottavio on the right and Alessandro on the left.

The seating area had 14 rows and a high baseline in a semi-oval plan. This was an innovation with respect to the conventional semi-circle plan (borrowed from classical models) that we find in Palladio's Teatro Olimpico at Vicenza (1589-90). Aleotti's conception offered not only greater seating capacity. It also corrected the distortions in view from the ends, thereby becoming a precursor of the horseshoe design that was to be universally adopted in the public theatres of the 18th and 19th centuries.

In the centre of the orchestra, but above the entrance, was the prince's balcony, forerunner of the «royal box». Above the orchestra seating are two tiers of loggias — the first Doric, the second Ionic — formed by serlianas (obviously borrowed from Palladio's ba-

silica at Vicenza). Both the loggias and upper level o attic had to be at least partially utilizable so as to ex tend upwards the space reserved for spectators (an ir timation of the tiered boxes in modern theatres).

The area reserved for the seats (benches in othe theatres) was in the Farnese theatre used as well fo staging. This, coupled with the Baroque settings tha projected beyond the stage's confines, abolished th separation of stage and audience.

The stage is indeed the real innovation of the Teatr Farnese. Thanks to ingenious mechanisms, uppe galleries for movement and a below stage area de signed for handling the mechanisms, the first, tru mobile settings in the history of the theatre had thei debut on the Farnese stage. The imposing proscen ium, with its giant Corinthian order, marked the cor fines of the sets and hid from the audience the comple machinery (no longer extant) that created them.

Above the Farnese coat of arms in the centre is th dedicatory inscription to the Muses: BELLONAE (reference to the military function of the original hal AC MUSIS THEATRUM RAYNUTIUS FARNE SIUS PARMAE AC PLACENTIAE DUX IV CAS TRI V AUGUSTA MUNIFICENTIA APERUIT AN NO MDCXIX.

The theatre's decoration — the illusionistic pe spectives and ornamental motifs on the auditorium walls and the statues, almost all completely destroye — are the works of many artists: the painters Lionell Spada and Girolamo Curti of Bologna, G.B. Trotti o Cremona («Malosso»), and Sisto Badalocchio an Antonio Bertoja of Parma; and the stucco master who were led by Luca Reti of Ticino, the artist of th two equestrian statues of the triumphal arches.

By the end of 1618 the theatre was completed but Cosimo's visit had in the meantime been can celled. The theatre had to wait another ten year (1628) before being officially inaugurated. Th occasion: the long-awaited marriage of Odoard and Margherita. The spectacle (probably masque) written by Achillini and scored b Monteverdi, was a veritable display of scenic vii tuosity; it even included a «naumachia» (moc naval battle) that required the flooding of the en tire space in front of the seating area.

Despite this impressive beginning, the theatr did not live up to expectations. It was used onl sporadically. Thereafter, and then, only for spe cial occasions — almost always a wedding — tha had the power to attract a large aristocratic audience to the celebrations of a declining court.

The Teatro Farnese closed its doors in 1732, after the last spectacle held in honour of the arrival of the new duke, Charles of Bourbon, in Parma. As the era of the court theatre came to an end, victim of new social and technical demands, the age of the large-scale public theatre, borne on the wings of new design techniques, began to dawn.

Hours: Tues-Sat 9am-2pm, Sundays & Holidays 9am-1pm. Closed Mondays.

THE GALLERIA NAZIONALE

Parma's artistic patrimony had been the result of Farnese patronage and collecting. The core of this collection was first housed in the Palazzo del Giardino, whence it was removed to the Pilotta. It was later taken from Parma itself and transferred in toto to Naples by Charles of Bourbon, son of Elisabetta Farnese and heir to the duchy, who had become King of the Two Sicilies. He even went so far as to take the furnishings of the royal residences along with the works of art.

Among the paintings that were spirited to Capodimonte were Correggio's Gypsy Girl and the Mystical Union of St Catherine, Parmigianino's Antea and Portrait of Galeazzo Sanvitale, and others by Lorenzo Lotto, Titian, Sebastiano del Piombo, El Greco, Raphael, Dosso Dossi, Bertoja, Rondani, Anselmi, Lelio Orsi, Lanfranco, Schedoni and Bruguel.

The new Duke Philip tried to fill in the rather gaping holes left by his brother. As part of his Enlightenment policies under the direction of Du Tillot, he instituted the Accademia delle Belle Arti (Fine Arts Academy) in the Pilotta to promote artistic endeavours. He also founded a new art collection (to be built round Correggio's Madonna di San Gerolamo from the Church of St Anthony) to foster the education of the academy's students.

Duke Ferdinando added to the collection begun by his father. He acquired, among others, Marchese Taccoli Canacci's collection of Tuscan primitives (1786-1787).

Parma's collection was again carried off, this time by Napoleon (although many but not all of these works returned with Marie Louise's arrival at Parma in 1816). It was indeed Marie Louise herself, with the help of Paolo Toschi, who added to the collection. They acquired the private collections of the Sanvitales, Callanis, Baiardis, Rossis and the Dalla Rosa Pratis. These pur-

Galleria Nazionale. Correggio. Madonna di S. Girolamo.

Correggio. The Annunciation.

Galleria Nazionale. North wing.

the architect Guido Canali, and work is now at an advanced stage.

The Gallery has devoted special attention to Correggio and Parmigianino. They even have a reserved section in the «Rocchetta», which preserves the historical context of the works as planned by Toschi and Bettoli.

Correggio's works include the removed frescos of the Madonna della Scala, the Virgin Enthroned, and the Annunciation; the paintings of the Deposition, the Martyrdom of Four Saints, the Madonna della Scodella and the Madonna di S. Girolamo. The latter work, displaying Correggio's mature style, is the most important. It became a model of painting in the Emilia for centuries thereafter as well as being emblematic of the National Gallery itself.

There are only two works by Parmigianino in the Gallery: the so-called Turkish Slave Girl (an example of the artist's striving for perfection and exalted beauty) and a small Self-portrait on paper, with a signed pen ink drawing on the back.

Through the imposing «entrance» provided by the Teatro Farnese, the visit to the Gallery continues (the works are ordered chronologically and by school).

chases were then exhibited in orderly arrangement in the Pilotta, where rooms were newly refurnished and specifically laid out by the architect Nicola Bettoli.

The Gallery (the «National» dates to 1945) became independent of the Fine Arts Academy in 1882. It was to undergo a succession of remodellings and alterations thereafter. The two most important of these occurred in 1938-39 (new methods in museography) and in 1967. The latter involves a radical alteration and remodelling that will affect the entire length of the palazzo that faces the north side of the «Guazzatoio» quadrangle. The project plans were drawn up by

1. National Picture Gallery. Benvenuto Tisi called Garofalo. Madonna and Child. 2. Correggio. Madonna of the bowl. 3. Doors of S. Bertoldo (detail) 10-11th cent. 4. Leonardo da Vinci. Young girl's head. 5. Parmigianino. Portrait of young woman called the Turkish slave.

84

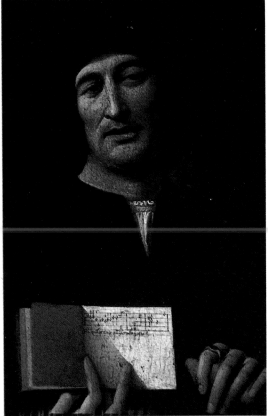

gilt background of the 14th and 15th centuries. Included are the triptych of the Crucifixes by Simone, an artist whose distinctive «Po valley» style sets him apart from such Tuscan contemporaries as Spinello Aretino, Agnolo Gaddi, Beato Angelico and Giovanni di Paolo.

An interesting series of ceramic tiles adorned with figures and plant motifs provides a rare glimpse of late 15th-century floor decoration (from the abolished convent of St Paul, probably the cell of St Catherine).

One of the Gallery's masterpieces is the beautiful «Chiaroscuro» sketch of a young girl's head by Leonardo da Vinci.

Veneto Renaissance painting is represented by four works of Cima da Conegliano, including two poetic tondi of mythological theme.

Roman painting is represented by Sebastiano del Piombo's unfinished portrait of Clement VII.

Painting in the Emilia is a section that includes 15th- and 16th-century works by Jacopo Loschi, Cristoforo Caselli, Francesco Raibolini («Francia»), Josaphat and Alessandro Araldi, the Mazzolas and the Mannerist Michelangelo Anselmi, Giorgio Gandini del Grano and Girolamo Bedoli. Of this latter, Parmigianino's heir in terms of style, noteworthy are the Conception and Parma embracing Alessandro Farnese (the other portrait of the young duke is by the Fleming Anthonis Mor).

A significant example of Italian Mannerism is El Greco's small painting of the Healing of a Blind Man.

Late 16th- and 17th-century painting in the Emilia: The Deposition by Annibale Carracci, the two splendid works by Bartolomeo Schedoni of Modena that stand out for their theatricality of gesture and pervading metallic light effects, Giovanni Lanfranco's St Agatha in prison being cared for by St Peter, the two paintings by Guercino, P.F. Cittadini's Portrait of a Young Girl, and works by Burrini, Cignani and G.M. Crespi.

Another important section is dedicated to 17th-century Genoese, Spanish and Flemish art, with paintings by G.A. De Ferrari, Murillo and A. Van Dyck.

Genre painting of the 17th and 18th centuries includes works by Boselli, Munari and Spolverini.

18th-century Veneto painting has works by Tiepolo, Pittoni, Piazzetta, Canaletto, Bellotto and Ricci

The Medieval section. The Gallery collections proper begin here. Included are the fine carved wooden doors (10th-11th centuries) of San Bertoldo, capitals bearing historical scenes, and a panel with the Majestas Domini by Benedetto Antelami (supposed to have originally been part of the Duomo's chancel arch or pulpit).

The next section. This is dedicated to paintings on

1. National Picture Gallery. Piero di Puccio. Triptych with Enthroned Madonna and Child with Saints. 2. Domenico Theotocopuli called El Greco. The healing of the blind. 3. Filippo Mazzola. Portrait of a musician. 4. Bartolomeo Schedoni. The three Marys at the Sepulchre. 5. G.B. Cima da Conegliano. Endymion asleep. 6. Filippo Mazzola. Christ carrying the Cross.

6

that provide a good background history to Parma's painting before the Bourbon collection.

The large portrait of Don Filippo Bourbon and Family in the «Marie Louise» room signals a change in Parma's artistic tastes. This new period of «internationalism», as shown in the works of P. Ferrari, Benigno Bossi, Zoffany, Natier, Le Brun, Doyen and the numerous academic painters from Italy and other European countries, will begin to narrow in scope towards the late 1700s with the rise of devotional works (although the artistic quality remains high, as can be seen in the paintings of G. Peroni and G. Callani).

The Marie Louise period includes a sculpture of the duchess by A. Canova, the portraits by Borghesi, Appiani, Biagio Martini and G.A. Pock, and the landscapes by G. Boccaccio and G. Drugman.

The closing sections exhibit works from the second half of the 19th century, including those by Cletofonte Preti, Guido Cermignani, Salvatore and Luigi Marchesi and Cecrope Barilli — painters who by and large express a more intimate view of life and art.

Hours: Tues-Sat 9am-2pm, Sundays & Holidays 9am-1pm. Closed Mondays.

1. Galleria Nazionale. Jacopo Zanguidi, called il Bertoja. The Judgement of Paris, fresco coming from a room of the Palazzo Giardino. 2. Giovanni Antonio Canal, called il Canaletto. Ideal view with the Basilica of Vicenza. 3. Giovanni Francesco Barbieri, called il Guercino. Susanna and the old men. 4. Bernardo Bellotto. Arch of Titus. 5. Giuseppe Baldrighi. Don Filippo di Borbone with his family (detail).

BIBLIOTECA PALATINA

Instituted in 1761, just one year following the creation of the Museum of Antiquities, the Palatine Library was another prominent part of Philip of Bourbon's enlightened cultural policy as practised by Du Tillot. It, too, is housed in the Pilotta complex. Destined for public use from its very inception, the Library was first known under the name «Regia Biblioteca Parmense»; the «Palatine» appellation was bestowed in 1865 when the Library became the repository of the Bourbon collection of valuable manuscripts and printed books.

The curator of the Library was Paolo Maria Paciaudi of Turin (1710-85), Theatin father, scholar and antiquarian, who was summoned to Parma by the duke to organise the library.

Opposite the entrance is the room housing the solid walnut antique furnishings (partly rebuilt); they were crafted from designs by the duke's architect, Ennemond Alexandre **Petitot**. In the **Galleria dell'Incoronata** is preserved the sinopia (fresco underdrawing) of the central group of the fresco Correggio executed for the original apse vault of the Church of St John the Evangelist.

THE «SALA DANTE». The fine wooden bookcases house the Ortalli Collection, one of Italy's largest collections of prints. The Dante room derives its name from the encaustic-wax pictures on the walls that depict scenes from the poet's *Divine Comedy*. The artist was Francesco Scaramuzza of Parma, who executed them from 1841 to 1857.

SALA MARIA LUIGIA. The large Marie Louise reading room is actually in an annex independent of the Pilotta but abutting it on the south side; it was so designed by Nicola Bettoli in 1834. The walls are adorned by book-cases with stucco ornamentation painted to simulate marble in the neoclassical style. The fresco of the tunnel vaulting, with its coffers and figure-decorated medallions, was executed by Francesco Scaramuzza, Giovanni Gaibazzi, Stanislao Campana and other academic artists.

The books in the library's collection number 700,000 volumes, including 5,000 manuscripts, 50,000 autographs, 3,000 incunabola and 50,000 engravings mostly from the Ortalli collection.

Hours: Mon-Thurs 8.30am-7pm, Fri-Sat 8.30am-1.30pm. Closed Sundays.

MUSEO BODONIANO

Founded in 1963, the «Bodoni Museum» is housed on the top floor of the Palatine Library. As its name suggests, it is dedicated to Giambattista Bodoni (1740-1813), engraver, typographer and publisher, who was invited to Parma from his native Saluzzo by duke Ferdinand of Bourbon in 1768 to establish and direct the «Stamperia Reale» (Royal Printing Press).

Celebrated as the inventor of the Bodoni typeface as well as for his superbly printed and bound editions, Bodoni made the press one of the most famous in the world at that time.

The collection includes works printed by the master in his type-face, the tools of his art: punches, original dies, characters, printing frames and other objects used in melting lead. There are, in addition, manuscripts and books from Italian and foreign printers illustrating the development of printing as well as works devoted to printing at Parma.

The Bodoni Museum also has a library containing an interesting collection of Bodoni's personal papers.

MONUMENTO A BOTTEGO

This was one of the first monuments designated to upgrade one of the city's marginal, deteriorating areas that had since been slated for renewal with the building of the railway in 1859. Made of bronze and stone by Ettore Ximenes of Palermo in 1907, the memorial was erected on the 10th anniversary of the death of Vittorio Bottego of Parma, a famous explorer of Africa. Garbed in the uniform of the colonial troops, his figure rises from a stone spur flanked below by two African warriors symbolising the Omo and Giuba rivers the waters of which flow into the large circular pool.

1

1. Palatina Library. Maria Luigia's room. 2. A. Dalla Chiesa Square. Monument of Vittorio Bottego. 3. Toschi Avenue. Monument of the Victory: project of L. Cusani, bronze parts by E. Ximenes (1931). Garibaldi Street. Oratory of Rossi. The front (XIX century).

4

PARCO E PALAZZO DUCALE

It was Ottavio, the first Farnese duke to establish permanent residence at Parma, who commissioned the Palazzo and landscaping of the Park in the surrounding greenery in 1561. This is the first of the many real property development initiatives undertaken by the Farneses. For, it must be remembered, that Parma had suddenly become the duchy's capital and was woefully lacking in both suitable buildings and the decorum befitting the role it was now called upon to play.

Indeed, when the court first installed itself at Parma, it was forced to reside in the old Palazzo Vescovile or bishop's residence. Thereafter, it chose a number of already existing palazzi to serve its needs. These were connected one to the other and situated between the present-day Via Cavour and Piazzale della Pace — certainly not what one would expect of the ruling family, given the fact that these palazzi did anything but stand out from the surrounding cityscape.

The Palazzo del Giardino. Designed originally to be the duke's representative seat and residence, thereby solving the chronic lack of one, the Garden Palace was also intended as the family's summer residence, since it was located at the out-

skirts of the city proper. Its construction was also part of Ottavio's policy of creating the proper dignity and decorum in Parma's cityscape. This was why the site chosen was one in the rather shabby «cross-river» («Oltretorrente») area that had few buildings and those were mainly dwellings of the poorer classes.

The duke purchased the large tract of land from private owners (where once had stood the Sforza castle with the river up against its walls) as well as the Renaissance Palazzetto Eucherio Sanvitale. He then commissioned the architect Vignola (Jacopo Barozzi) of Modena to landscape the garden area and design the residence.

THE PARK or garden, originally laid out in typically Italian fashion, was altered many times and radically through the centuries. In 1690, as part of the grandiose setting created to celebrate a Farnese wedding, the large fish pond closing off what is now the main avenue was installed. **The three-tier fountain** at its centre came from the Colorno Palazzo in 1920; it is called the «Fountain of Trianon» after that designed for one of the buildings at Versailles.

Following a period of decline, Philip of Bourbon decided to revive the garden's fortunes towards the mid-1700s. The court architect E.A. Petitot drew up the landscape plans from a design based on French models and sent directly from France by Contant d'Ivry. To this period also belongs the erection of the «tempietto» or small temple, which was built as an artificial ruin according to the prevailing taste of the day. It is located to the right of the main avenue in the centre of the woods; though now destroyed, it once hosted the meetings of the Academy of Arcadia members.

Petitot is also credited with the gate facing Santa

---

1. *Parco Ducale. 2. The fountain called Trianon. 3. The Little Temple of Arcadia.*

Croce and, presumably, the other one on the Strada Farnese (both still in existence). J.B. Boudard also contributed to the French atmosphere by sculpting from 1753 to 1766 numerous statues and group sculptures after models drawn from those in the gardens of the French court. They are still extant. To the right of the main entrance is his finest piece: the Silenus group designed for the Arcadia woods. Another

1. Parco Ducale. J.B. Boudard. The Sileno group. 2. J.B. Boudard. Pomona. 3. The Palace of the Garden.

2

ur statues, tastefully set in front of the Palazzo, depict the divinities of the fields: Vertumnus and Pomona to the right, Pale and Triptolemus to the left. Additional statues representing mythological figures are to be found along the roads flanking the garden.

During the era of Marie Louise, what had been a secluded and intimate garden given to the pleasures and leisure of the courtiers now became a public place, taking on a more naturalistic, «English» air.

The grounds of the Palazzo also were the site of an 0-metre long «Aranciaia» or orange grove and a splendid orchard of exotic tree species. Both were destroyed at the beginning of the 20th century, as were the old city walls. The walls had once run along the north and west sides of the garden for some distance and, since it was possible to walk the promenade atop the bastions, provided the amenity of a pleasant panoramic stroll with an overview of the garden. Since the garden became the property of the city in 1866, it has substantially preserved the appearance it had during the era of Marie Louise.

PALAZZO DEL GIARDINO. Like the garden, so the palazzo no longer preserves its 16th-century appearance. Built on the site of the old Sforza fortress, it, too, underwent substantial alterations during the 17th and 18th centuries.

As designed by Vignola, the original edifice corresponds (in the present-day palazzo) to the central cube-shaped part with tower and side wings. It is also missing many of its distinguishing features: the two marble stairways (right and left) leading up to the main entrance on the «piano nobile» or main floor, where the balcony with bal-

95

ustrade is now; the richly decorated grotto below (where the main entrance is today) that was wedged into the ground floor; and, in the area directly in front of the façade, Giovanni Boscoli da Montepulciano's stately fish pond-fountain that was adorned with statues and a bridge across its centre leading to the palazzo.

By 1600, apart from its striking picturesqueness, Vignola's palazzo must have appeared a bit too small. Thus the alterations. Two courtyards on either side of the central cube and two foreparts projecting from the façade were added, giving the building a plan in the form of an «H» that one sees today. These changes, which made it necessary to demolish the stairways and the extravagant fountain, were in all likelihood planned by Moschino and Rainaldi, the latter of whom also designed the Baroque cornices framing the main floor's windows.

There were other alterations during the age of the Bourbons. In 1767, E.A. Petitot added the grand interior staircase, the mezzanine in the two façade wings and raised the front foreparts by a floor. His, too, are the neoclassical friezes adorning some of the windows.

Since then, there have been no further substantial changes. In fact, it was little used either by the Bourbons or Marie Louise, who preferred the palazzi at Colorno and Sala as summer residences. Today, painted that «Parma yellow» as popular with the Bourbon court as with Petitot, who used it wherever possible, it is the station of the Carabinieri (state police).

The interior. The 18th-century staircase leads to the central room of the main floor. It is called the «sala degli uccelli» or birds' room because of the 204 stucco bird figures by the sculptor Benigno Bossi of Varese, who executed them between 1766 and 1767.

One can proceed from here to the four rooms that still feature (albeit only traces in some instances) what remains of the Farnese decorations. Already damaged to considerable extent by Petitot, they were subsequently subjected to whitewashing, actually a form of censorship in this case, by the extremely prudish Ferdinand of Bourbon, who must have found the figures of «nude women» of 16th- and 17th-century art rather unspeakable. Now that subsequent restorations have again brought these pictures into the light of day, they clearly show the highly refined taste and erudition of the Farnese court. The figures are obviously inspired by and drawn from the chivalric romances and fantastic tales of mythology then in vogue at the princely courts. That such themes were meant to decorate the palazzo where the duke frequently spent his leisure hours in pleasurable pursuits further serves to underscore the cultural atmosphere of Parma at the time.

THE FIRST ROOM in chronological order is the one at the back to the left. It was decorated ca. 1568-70 by Girolamo Mirola of Bologna and Bertoja (Jacopo Zanguidi), a mannerist of Parma. By an erroneous interpretation of its iconography or meaning, it was originally thought that the pictorial representation were drawn from the tale of Orpheus. In actual fact however, they depict the meeting between Ruggero and the sorceress Alcina that is found in Canto VII o Ariosto's Orlando Furioso.

The tale begins on the west wall (immediately to the left of the entrance) as Ruggero arrives and is greeted by Alcina against a background of an arcade with well-appointed table. The scene then shifts to the north wall: the «lighthearted game» of damsels and knights and their pages who, beyond a column adorned with figures and through a window, can be seen leading the guests to their rooms. The scenes remaining on this wall and those depicted on the following ones are extraneous to the tale and were executed at later dates.

Ariosto's tale continues, however, on the vault about the central panel, which probably portrayed the amorous encounter between the knight and the sorceress, are depicted the delightful pursuits of Alcina' guests (dancing, bathing, hunting, and so on) and the two lovers reading, according to the poem, «the amorous tales of the ancients».

«SALA DEL BACIO». «The room of the kiss» or «o Aetas Felicior», it was probably executed by Bertoja alone, as Mirola had died in 1570. Crowned by a cornice bearing the inscription «AETAS FELICIOR the central panel depicts the foreground figure of a nude woman accompanied by an old man and a young one embracing her: she is voluptuousness, who dominates all the ages of man. The old man with the scythe on clouds portrayed in the lefthand corner is Saturn symbolising the mythical golden age, the happiest of all.

All round and on the walls are the scenes drawn from another tale of chivalry, this time from Boiardo' poem, Orlando Innamorato. They tell the story of Orlando's liberation. He has been the victim of a magic spell and is a prisoner in the Crystal Palace, beneath the «river of laughter». The vault shows other knights the hero's companions, being guided by Fiordelisa who is thoroughly versed in the magic arts, as they set out to rescue him. After crossing an enchanted forest they reach the river beneath which (the tale continues on the walls) is the Palace, superbly pictured with it crystal columns framing the scene of the kiss and the lost knights (south wall). Once the spell is lifted, the knights are seen floating on the river as they make for the bank (west wall).

Surmounting the scenes on the walls is the Virgilian verse (mistakenly transcribed): «TRAHETAS SUA QUEMQUE / VOLUPTAS» «to each his own».

From the first room it is possible to visit a small room on the left containing two fragments of a complete pictorial cycle. The scenes are drawn from Tasso's Gerusalemme Liberata and portray the adventures of Erminia. The work was probably painted by Alessandro Tiarini of Bologna (ca. 1628).

---

1. Palazzo del Giardino. Hall of Aetas Felicior. Bertoja. Detail of the frescoes of the vault.

The last room on the left, called the «Sala dell'Amore» or «room of love», was begun ca. 1601 by Agostino Carracci, who also did the vault scenes portraying allegories of love: in the central octagon, «Three Amorini Preparing the Bow» (venal love); right, «Aeneas at the Ship's Bow with Venus» (chaste love); left, «Venus and Mars by a Jetty» (wanton love); over the window, «Peleus and Thetis with Her Body Hidden by Fish Scales» (love of virtue). In the fifth panel, which was left bare because of Carracci's death, there is an inscription in his memory.

The stucco decorations that continue the mythological love themes are by Luca Reti. The decorations were continued on the walls, too, towards the end of the 1600s by Carlo Cignani of Bologna, who rendered

them as though they were paintings: from the left «The Seduction of Europa», «The Triumph of Venus and Amor with the Graces and Pleasure», «Bacchus Offering Ariadne the Treasure», «Apollo and Daphne», and «The Conflict Between Amor and Pan».

In one of the rooms in the wing opposite the main floor are the only surviving examples of the numerous paintings that Malosso (Giovan Battista Trotti) executed in the palazzo. They are the scenes (1604) on three of the walls depicting: «Jupiter Meeting Bacchus and Venus», «The Sacrifice of Alcestis» and «Circe Changing the Swine Back into Ulysses' Companions». The two landscapes flanking either side of the window on the south wall are by the Fleming J. Sons.

PALAZZETTO EUCHERIO SANVITALE. A fine example of Renaissance architecture at Parma, this moderately sized palazzetto or «small palace» is located nearby the garden's secondary entrance.

Antedating the Farnese buildings in this area, the palazzetto was erected ca. 1520 and reputedly designed by the architect Giorgio da Erba, one of the most prominent in the city at the time. The owner was Scipione Dalla Rosa, who probably also had it commissioned. He later sold the building to monsignor Eucherio Sanvitale, who used it as a place of appointment for private receptions of the aristocracy. His priestly coat of arms once

appeared above the mottos over the jambs of the doors on the west and east sides of the edifice.

The Palazzetto Sanvitale was thereafter sold to Ottavio Farnese. Set in the surrounding gardens that he purchased at the same time, Ottavio used the building as an auxiliary guest residence; later, first under the Bourbons and then Marie Louise, the palazzetto went through a series of alterations and was used as the residence of the grounds' keepers.

Recently reopened following a lengthy series of restoration works, the Palazzetto has regained a semblance of its original appearance, which includes such distinctive features as the H-shaped floor plan, the four corner towers of the two main wings (east and west), and the loggias (five arches supported by sandstone columns).

Gian Francesco d'Agrate probably executed the stone decorations; those of the two-light mullion windows on the ground floors of the towers are particularly worthy of note.

The interior. These rooms are now used for exhibitions and are open to the public only during the actual shows.

However, the 16th-century pictorial decorations, which were brought to light after centuries beneath

whitewash, proved to be of great interest. Unfortunately, the restoration was only able to recover them in part.

The first room (to the right of the entrance). The recovered art work here includes fragments of a lunette depicting the Madonna and Child by Parmigianino; an umbrella vault with late 16th-century frescos covers the adjoining room. This room leads to another, very small, which originally was a chapel. Here the restorers did an excellent job. They uncovered a splendid cycle of oil wall paintings portraying (today in a rather fragmentary manner) scenes from the life of the Virgin. The paintings also reveal the hand of a truly talented, late-mannerist artist influenced by northern styles. The name most recently put forth is that of father Cosmo da Castelfranco (Paolo Piazza), who was known to be in Parma during the first decade of the 17th century.

1. Palazzo del Giardino. Hall of Aetas Felicior. Bertoja. Detail of the frescoes of the vault. 2. Hall of Love. Frescoes with «Triumph of Venus and Love with the Graces and Pleasure» and Bacchus offering the treasure to Arianne. 3. Duke's Park. The Renaissance Palazzetto Eucherio Sanvitale. 4. Parmigianino. Fragments of fresco with Madonna and Child.

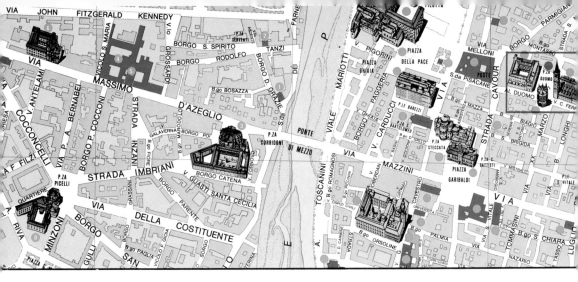

TOUR NO. 4

ORATORIO DI SANTA MARIA DELLE GRAZIE

Begun 1617 to hold a supposedly miraculous picture of Our Lady of Mercy, a late 16th-century work by an unknown local painter, the oratory falls into the Oltretorrente («cross-river») style promoted by the early Farnese dukes.

On the basis of its particular structure, this central-plan church with two side chapels and a large central presbytery is ascribed to Giovan Battista Magnani, court architect.

In 1644 the building was renovated by Geronimo Rainaldi of Rome, who also added the octagonal lantern over the presbytery and moved the main entrance to the east side, thereby modifying the distribution of the interior spaces.

The interior, rhythmically accented by columns with capitals decorated in a gilt-shell motif, has refined Rococo illusionistic quadrature, deep perspec-

tives and assorted ornamental elements by the Cremonese perspective artist Francesco Natali (1715).

The elegant figures of angels and putti that so marvelously people these frescos, like that of the cupola, were clearly influenced by Correggio in their composition. They depict in ethereal celestial glory the Assumption of the Virgin and the prophets Isaiah, Samson, David and Daniel in the pendentives. Painted in 1715 by Sebastiano Galeotti, an excellent fresco artist with a quick lively hand, the refined and delicate colouring is in shades of pale yellow, grey and blue.

In the **sanctuary**, which scenically recedes towards the ambulatory, one finds the oil on wood painting of Our Lady of Mercy, transferred to the church in 1621

The excellent choir stalls in carved, gilded wood date to the early 17th century, while the multi-coloured marble altar is 18th century.

The painted terracotta group with a lifeless Christ supported by an angel and located under the altar is by Giuseppe Sbravati (1743-1818).

In the chapel on the right there is a painting by Antonio Savazzini (1766-1822) portraying the Holy Family with St Francis, while the chapel on the left holds a 1621 altarpiece with a guardian angel attributed to Sisto Badalocchio.

TOSCANINI HOUSE

Near the Oratorio di S. Maria delle Grazie, in one of the typical quarters of Oltretorrente, you can visit the native house of the famous Maestro Arturo Toscanini (Parma 1867 - New York 1957), a modest house, recently renewed, where there're shown relics belonging to the musician.

In 1876, when he was nine, Toscanini entered the Music Royal School of the town, in 1885 he graduated with full marks in violoncello, after testing himself as composer.

His bright career as orchestra conductor began for a fortuitous event in 1886 in Rio de Janeiro, where the young 'cellist, member of the Italian orchestra on tour in South America, had to substitute the Brazilian conductor in the conduction of Aida. From now on, Toscanini made himself known in the most important European and American theatres, becoming more famous than any other conductor.

1. Oratory of S. Maria delle Grazie. Interior. 2. Giacomo Grosso. Portrait of A. Toscanini. 3. Façade of A. Toscanini's Birthhouse. 4. City cemetery of «La Villetta». Tomb of N. Paganini.

101

After conducting the Scala orchestra from 1898 to 1928, during Fascism, Toscanini moved to the United States, conducting the most important orchestras in New York, where he died after intermittent returns in Italy.

Walking in the first little avenue on the left of «La Villetta», the town cemetery, you can see the neoclassic grave of the great musician Niccolò Paganini (1782-1840).

He died in Nice and in 1876 his mortal remains were sent to Parma, the town where he worked as a member Supervisor of the court orchestra during the Dukedom of Maria Luigia and where he had a villa, situated at Gaione, few kilometres far from Parma.

SANTISSIMA ANNUNZIATA

In 1470 Rolando II Pallavicino made a huge donation to the construction of this monastery of Friar Minor Conventuals in the southern part of the city outside the town-walls. The complex included this church where Correggio painted an Annunciation in a lunette.

The reinforcement of fortifications carried out by the Duke Pier Luigi entailed the church's demolition (1546) and the transfer of the friary within the walls at Capo di Ponte near the Pietra Bridge. Under the Farnese policy of beautification and development of the Oltretorrente area, it was decided that a new church and a Franciscan monastery would be built on this site. Work began in 1566 on a plan by Giovan Battista Fornovo — Vignola's collaborator in the Palazzi Farnese at Piacenza and Caprarola — as pre-

sumed by stylistic comparisons between this and the church of San Quintino.

Following Vignola's example, Fornovo adopted an oval plan with radial chapels for the church, but came up with an original architectonic solution by placing the entrance on the major axis instead of the minor one, thus creating one of the most significant monuments of experimental Emilian Mannerism of the late 16th century.

The exterior of the building is characterized by an imposing mass emphasised by a large central arch crowned with a pediment and flanked by two side arches that bring to mind the façade of Sant'Andrea at Mantua by Leon Battista Alberti.

The sequence of the ten chapels gives the body of the building a lively spatial articulation accentuated by the intervening buttressed columns. Their decoration, with small niches on fluted shelves at the top under which open windows with tympana moved by a speartip-shaped quoin, is excessively anticlassical and properly Mannerist.

The three architectural orders emphasizing the façade unify and connect the building's structure.

Above the 17th-century entry portal is the majestic stucco group amid clouds and angels that recall Correggio portraying the Eternal Father and the Annunciation, done shortly after 1680 by the Lombard Giovan Battista Barberini and commissioned by the Friars Minor, as the coat of arms on the architrave attests

The oval interior is extended longitudinally by the large choir located beyond the triumphal arch of the chancel.

The construction of the barrel vault (1627-32) was directed by Geronimo Rainaldi of Rome, who finished Fornovo's project.

The Annunciation relief in the open-base tympanum of the triumphal arch, the four statues of Franciscan saints and the refined stucco decoration of the frieze with putti and foliate motifs were executed between 1632 and 1634 by the brothers Giovan Battista and Luca Reti from Laino, exponents of a style still tied to 16th-century Mannerism, as is also evident in Luca's work at the Teatro Farnese.

The altarpiece in the first chapel on the right depicting the Virgin and Child and saints merits particular attention. It is the work of Pier Antonio Bernabei of Parma, known as della Casa (1567-1630). In the second chapel there is the painting of St Bonaventure kneeling before the Virgin by Sebastiano Galeotti dating to ca. 1720.

The main altarpiece depicting the Virgin enthroned and Child with saints (1518) is by the Romagna artist Francesco Zaganelli from Cotignola, to whom the portraits of Rolando II Pallavicino with daughter and wife, Domitilla Gambara, set in the plinths of the Late Baroque altarpiece are attributed In addition to these works, a wooden choir by an unknown carver from the old-15th century church has the central back stall panels decorated with the Pallavicino coat of arms flanked by that of the Franciscan order.

Stylistic comparisons permit the stucco ornamentation of the vault and the statues of St Peter of Alcantara and a Franciscan saint in niches in the fourth chapel on the left after entering to be attributed to Luca Reti. The frescos on the vault facing depicting episodes in the life of St Peter of Alcantara are the work of Ilario Spolverini (1657-1734) from Parma, a Farnese court painter to whom the altarpiece with this saint is also attributed.

Still on the left, in the third chapel, one finds the statues of St John the Evangelist and the prophet Isaiah by the Parmesan artist Gaetano Callani (1765).

Of note in the building's vestibule is a 19th-century copy by the Parmesan academy painter Ignazio Affanni (1828-89) of Correggio's fresco, the Annunciation, presently in the National Gallery.

The large **cloister** attributed to Fornovo against the southern side of the building was begun at the same time as the church and completed only in 1688 after a troubled history of construction problems. It comprised an arcade topped by a gallery that was closed off in the early 18th century to accommodate the friars' cells.

In 1637 the architect Giovan Battista Magnani designed the refectory vault.

Rare religious volumes are preserved in a well-endowed **library** that forms part of the monastery complex.

The Franciscan Padre Lino led an exemplary life here. His unstinting charity helped the poor who lived across the river. Still beloved and prayed to by the faithful of Parma, he is commemorated by a funerary statue in the city cemetery.

OSPEDALE VECCHIO

Created in 1201 by Rodolfo Tanzi, reputedly a Knight of the Teutonic Order, out of some houses in Borgo Taschieri (today Borgo Coccoli), the hospital soon became too small to hold all the ill. It was rebuilt also to house foundlings (and for this reason was also known as «Esposti», Foundlings Hospital) ca. 1250 by the successor of a certain priest named Pietro on the north side of the main S. Croce road (today Via D'Azeglio).

When most of the smaller hospitals in Parma and the surrounding area were included in Tanzi's by Pope Sixtus IV's 1471 grant to the city's elderly, it was decided that a new hospital would be built on the site of the old one.

The new building, designed by Gian Antonio da Erba, who was probably assisted by a relative, Giovanni Giacomo da Erba until the former's death (1507-1508), was begun in 1476. In 1491 the construction of the ceiling and roofs was undertaken by the builder Gaspare Fatuli, who worked on the hospital until 1496-1497.

The building, which is the first important example of Renaissance architecture in Parma, was inspired by 15th-century Lombard models such as the Ospedale Maggiore in Milano by Filarete as well as Brunelleschi's Ospedale degli Innocenti in Florence. It was originally a large cross with only one of the four planned porticoed courtyards (on the south-east side) being completed. Its southern arm was given a facing that

1. Oratorio di S. Ilario. The interior. 2. Via M. D'Azeglio. The ex-Church of S. Francesco di Paola with its towers, called «dei Paolotti». 3. Church of S. Croce. Outside.

103

constituted its present façade along today's Via D'Azeglio. The hospital was not completed and later underwent a great deal of rebuilding. The patients and foundlings were housed in separate wards.

Part of the hospital's decoration was done by a painter called Geminiano from 1492 to 1501; Antonio Ferrari d'Agrate worked on the façade and the cloister from ca. 1491-1505.

The growing number of patients in the hospital, known at the time as the Ospedale della Misericordia (Mercy Hospital), and foundlings in the Ospizio degli Esposti, led to the first extension of the arms, perhaps the work of Gian Francesco Testa, in the late 16th century.

In 1663 the small Oratory of St Hilary was built at the entrance to the hospital's garden.

Blocks were added to the north ward in the first half of the 18th century. In 1758 the south arm was transformed from a church into a ward.

In 1782 Ferdinando I of Bourbon commissioned the extension of the north arm, as attested by the memorial stone above the entrance staircase. Also in 1782 J. Baptiste Cousinet, sculptor to the Duke, created the four stucco statues representing Compassion, Brotherly Love, Succor and Charity, which were originally located under the cupola where the arms cross and are now in the National Gallery.

The new façade and the staircase in the neoclassical style were designed in 1780 by the court architect Luigi Augusto Feneulle, while the wrought-iron gate with brass ornamentation is the work of Benedetto Galli (1784).

In 1843 Marie Louise decided to convert the west end of the hospital into living quarters for the Sisters of Charity; it was restructured to its present form probably by Nicola Bettoli.

In 1926 the patients were transferred to the new hospital at Prati di Valera. Since 1948 it has been the seat of the State Archives. Some of the rooms in the north-west wing are presently occupied by the City Library.

ORATORIO DI SANT'ILARIO

The oratory dedicated to St Hilary, the city's patron saint whose feast is January 13, was built in 1663 by order of Don Francesco Roncaglia, the director of the Ospedale della Misericordia (Mercy Hospital). The front has three portals: the largest is framed by two inset columns that support a high trabeation, while the two smaller portals are topped by lunettes depicting San Bovo as a knight on the left and San Nicomede as a priest and St Vincent wearing a dalmatic on the right.

The small interior is divided into a nave and two aisles by six square fluted columns with stucco capitals decorated with cherubs and animals on which the groin-vaults rest. The well-balanced pictorial decorations of plant festoons, saints, the beatified and putti against a trompe l'œil sky create an impression of uncommon charm.

These recently restored frescos depict the city's beatified and patron saints. They were painted between 1664 and 1666 by Giovan Maria Conti («della Camera») with the collaboration of Antonio Lombardi and Francesco Maria Reti. Conti, a member of Bernabei's school and still under the influence of the late 16-century Cremona style, also painted the fresco of Charity originally under the porticoes; it was removed in the last century and is now preserved in the

Pinacoteca (Picture Gallery).

The high wooden altar (late 17th century) comes from the Oratory of the Blessed Virgin and St James annexed to the Ospedale degli Incurabili (Incurables' Hospital) founded in the 14th century and administered by the Elders of the Four Arts (furriers, cobblers, butchers and smiths) whose insignia appear on the sides.

In a niche above is a 19th-century wooden statue of St Hilary.

On the right is a stone statue of this saint in bishop's robes with a kneeling worshipper, who perhaps commissioned the sculpture (15th century).

---

1. Church of Ss. Annunziata. Outside. 2. Via M. D'Azeglio. The porticos of the Ospedale Vecchio. 3. The front of the Ospedale Vecchio.

On the left is the funerary monument to Rodolfo Tanzi, who at the beginning of the 13th century founded what later became known as Ospedale della Misericordia (Mercy Hospital). It consists of a late 15th-century sarcophagus attributed to Antonio D'Agrate and a likeness of Tanzi on a clypeus or shield flanked by two stucco figures symbolizing Charity and Religion (1664-66), by Domenico Reti of Como, who also did the capitals of the oratory.

The low altar is dedicated to San Bovo.

The oratory is open to the public Saturday afternoons only.

SAN FRANCESCO DI PAOLA
(Torri dei Paolotti)

The imposing baroque façade and the two «Paolotti» towers flanking it were built in 1689 by the architect Carlo Virginio Draghi of Piacenza. They are all that remains of the monastery and church of the Minims of San Francesco di Paola built from 1625-32. In 1818 the complex became first an insane asylum and then a children's hospital; since 1936 it has been the University's science faculty.

SANTA CROCE

The building was erected about 1210 and was consecrated in 1222. It first underwent alteration in 1415 by architect Jorio da Erba. After the collapse of the vault over the high altar (1633), between 1635 and 1666 the nave (and aisles) were raised, the cupola was built and the large St Joseph's Chapel was added to the presbytery on the south side.

Between 1904 and 1909 new work was done to give the exterior back its Romanesque appearance. Remnants of the original structure can be seen in the floral pattern and animated chase of fantastic animals in the decorated portal and in the interior's columns and pillars crowned with decorative **capitals**. Outside Antelami's innovations, these archaic works appear in that almost forgotten «dialect» other examples of which can be found in the rustic parish churches strewn along the provincial Roman road of which S. Croce was the first stop outside the walls.

The capitals of the church reflect a still early Christian influence in the ornamental plant motifs, while the figurative elements draw their inspiration from the medieval bestiaries — that repertory of fantastic animals and monstrous, terrifying figures that populate Romanesque buildings.

life; Saint Joseph, the Virgin and the Holy Trinity are depicted on the ceiling, in ornamentation attributed to Alessandro Baratta.

Conti, who also executed the fresco decorations of the Capuchin Oratory and the entire cycle in the Oratory of Saint Hilary, reveals in his work strong ties with a 16th-century «Mannerist» style, while remaining almost indifferent to the naturalistic influence of 17-century Emilian painting.

SANTA MARIA DEL QUARTIERE

The church dedicated to the Virgin and known as «del Quartiere» (of the quarters) because it was built near military quarters, is a hexagon situated at a major crossroads, which gives it an unusual and imposing setting.

Its construction began in 1604 to house an image of the Madonna held to be miraculous. Initially financed by the Society of the Crucifix, which almost immediately abandoned the project as too big an undertaking, in 1610 it was taken over by the Third Regular Order of St Francis and completed in 1619.

The plan of the church exemplifies the exhilarating experiments on complex spatial compositions that were part of late 16th-century Emilian Mannerism. These became a major source in the following century for the intricate baroque creations of Guarino Guarini, who used the pagoda-like structure of S. Maria del Quartiere as a model in his work.

Local tradition attributes its design to Giovan Battista Aleotti of Ferrara («l'Argenta»), who also created the magnificent Farnese Theatre in Parma, or the architect Giovan Battista Magnani of Parma, or both, as is most likely.

Aleotti's original design was modified by

Possessing that strong plasticity that permeates Lombard sculpture, anatomically out of proportion, and executed with a certain crudeness, this work presents the peculiarities of a paradoxical expressionism. It includes wry smiles, vulgar leers and open-mouthed laughs that sometimes achieve humoristic and sarcastic effects, as in the first capital on the right: two peacocks are holding up by the ears a human mask (centre) that mocks the viewer with its protruding tongue.

The vast fresco decoration that adorns the nave, cupola (1634-37) and St Joseph's Chapel is the work of Giovanni Maria Conti.

Painted on the wall backing the façade is the Marriage Feast in Cana and, along the nave, are scenes of the Holy Family. The cupola features the Queen of Heaven amidst angelic musicians; in the pendentives are Sts Joachim, Elizabeth and John, a prophet and a sybil; in the arch is the Annunciation.

In St Joseph's chapel the walls depict scenes in his

1. Church of S. Croce. 3rd capital of the lower order on the left representing two fighters and a warrior. 2. Last capital of the lower order on the left representing a griffin and a dog. 3. Church of S. Maria del Quartiere. Outside.

Magnani in 1610, who enlarged the choir and created the monastery.

The church first appeared as a simple hexagonal prism with recessed rectangular chapels that were expanded at a later date (perhaps by Pietro Righini at the beginning of the 18th century) by three projecting parts connected by spatious passages forming an inner ambulatory (one original side can be seen to the south).

On the exterior, each side is characterized by windows with curved open-apex tympana flanked by pilaster-strips and rectangular and circular panel-work. A high trabeation with triglyphs connects the lower body, accented with massive angular columns, to the upper body, where the lightened buttresses take on a curved rhythm which gives the building its pagoda-like structure.

The hexagonal bell tower rises high to the south.

The interior's centre is dominated by a large cupola resting on angle pilaster-strips with shell capitals; the vaults of the chapels heighten and expand the spatial effect.

The innovative characteristics of architecture are of the greatest interest, which unfortunately cannot be said for the interior decoration. In any case, one should note the large ceiling fresco by Pier Antonio Bernabei (1626-1629) depicting Paradise with the Holy Spirit, the Holy Father, Jesus and the Virgin in a concentric splendour of saints. This is an emblematic example of both how Correggio's work on a large scale like the Duomo functions on a smaller one and how its innovation remained in the 17th century as local and limited rather than providing the impetus that elsewhere gave rise to the masterpieces of the Baroque.

In the drum appear the 1657 monochromatic figures of sybils and angels by Gian Maria Conti («della

Baiardi, who painted it in 1574 on the wall of the house in which he lived. It was removed in 1628 and brought to the church. The Virgin «del Quartiere» was also known as «dell'Abbondanza» (Virgin of plenty) from 1694, following a vow made to avert a famine. The decorations that run all around with putti among floral patterns and fruit is a 19th-century work by Francesco Scaramuzza of Parma (1803-1886).

Against the west side of the building is the monastery. It is an ample courtyard surrounded by a building where the Third Regular Franciscans resided until 1837, the year in which, following a cholera epidemic, the monastery was transformed into the Ospedale degli Incurabili (Incurables' Hospital), incorporating the 14th-century Ugolino Da Neviano Hospital. Today it houses clinics of the Ospedale Maggiore.

Camera»), who also painted the frescos in the second chapel on the right and the second on the left.

Imposing in their effect are the two majestic marble statues of the Madonna della Salute (ca. 1840) and St Louis, King of France (1841), with the latter being commissioned by Marie Louise to honour her patron saint. Both statues were done by the academy sculptor Tommaso Bandini of Parma.

The fresco behind the high altar with the Madonna nursing the Child and, on the right, St Francis in the act of prayer is the work of the Parmesan artist Mercurio

1. Church of S. Maria del Quartiere. P.A. Bernabei. The great fresco of the dome represents the Paradise. 2. Via della Salute (1856-1862). It's an important example of popular building wanted by Luisa Maria di Berry following the progressive town-planning that spread in Europe at the time. 3. Via Repubblica.

TOUR NO. 5

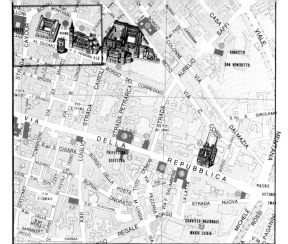

SAN VITALE

St Vitalis' Church was founded in the Middle Ages and refurbished in its present form between 1651 and 1658 by the architect Ficarelli (Cristoforo Rangoni). In 1676 the cupola was reinforced by the architect Domenico Valmagini.

The Latin-cross interior has a single nave flanked by four chapels on each side and a unique, impressive example of Emilian baroque sculpture in the left transept. The painting and sculpture-works belong to the **chapel of the Constantinople Madonna** commissioned by Carlo Beccaria, treasurer to the Farneses and prior of the Venerated Congregation of Suffrage, and were begun in 1627. The stuccos are by Domenico and Leonardo Reti, sons of Giovan Battista and grandsons of Luca Reti, ducal stucco masters from Como who executed them from 1666 to 1669.

The vast pictorial design is scenically developed in a vortex of whirling drapery, rejoicing putti, hovering angels, garlands of flowers and plants. It celebrates mainly the saints of the Beccaria family, whose crest — 13 mountains surmounted by an eagle — appears on the pendentives of the cupola, universal Piety, the Constantinople Madonna, protector of Christians subjugated by the Moslems, and the Congregation of Suffrage for the Souls in Purgatory.

The scene opens with the Blessed Tesauro Becca-

The altarpiece, the work of an unknown 17th-century Parmesan painter, depicts St Felix of Valois and St John of Matha bearing the Madonna of Constantinople.

Of considerable interest is the copy of Caravaggio's **Madonna** attributed to Carlo Francesco Nuvolone (*ca.* 1608-1660) in the second chapel on the right when entering.

The frescos narrating events in the life of St Vitalis in the apse are by Giuseppe Peroni (1763), who also did the canvas with the Madonna of Suffrage (1758) in the sacristy.

The high altarpiece of St Vitalis condemned to death is by Michele Plancher (1796-1848).

The third chapel on the left has a painting of the meeting of Louis XI and St Francis of Paola by Gaetano Callani, signed and dated 1799.

SAN QUINTINO

Founded as a church in the 9th century outside the town walls, it became in the 12th century a Benedictine convent that was abolished under Napoleonic rule. Only one of the three original cloisters is still to be seen in the courtyard of the adjacent house (street no. 25).

The church's most interesting feature is its distinctive architecture, which was completely redone in 1566 during the period in which it was governed by abbesses of the noble Sanvitale family. The new design was the work of G.B. Fornovo of Parma, an architect who collaborated with Vignola in the construction of the Farnese Palace at Caprarola, was superintendent of the Farnese Palace at Piacenza and designer of the important church of S.S. Annunziata in Parma itself.

The building clearly shows the features pecu-

ria holding the palm of martyrdom, left, and a side-long-rendering of the Blessed Francesco Beccaria, right. Both serve as the wings of the stage by directing the viewer's attention towards two other Beccaria family saints and Sts Andrea and Francis of Assisi amid clouds. At the base of the altarpiece, which is composed of a majestic, inscribed cartouche surmounted by a cross, one finds St Felix of Valois on the left and St John of Matha on the right. They founded the Order of the Trinity to ransom the Christian slaves held by the infidels and who were, therefore, their protectors, interceding with divine power to bring about their release that could be obtained only through Hope and Faith, portrayed as feminine figures on the right and left of the soffit, respectively. Another two virtues, Justice and Charity, which could be dispensed only by those of high rank, appear draped in their traditional flowing robes to the left and right of the window in the lunette crowned by the Paraclete. In the center of the arch two skeletal figures symbolize Death, the supreme judge of earthly matters according to the design of Providence.

These stuccos are a tableau informed with a vital, pulsating energy in endless, dynamic counterpoint to the pervasive and dominant baroque theme of «persuasion» — the persuasion of the faithful to devotion by means of captivating images. This is pursued here with typical Lombard vitality that denotes the Retis' profound debt to the early 17th-century painting of Cerano, Morazzone, Giulio Cesare Procaccini and Daniele Crespi.

ar to Fornova — the accentuated verticalism, the prevalence of the oval and ellipse, the heightened emphasis of the exterior walls, especially on the Borgo del Canale side, where the wall facing shows the interior subdivision of the chapels.

The interior. Before a major 19th-century alteration added the apse, it ended in a flat wall at the entry to the presbytery. The symmetrical, nave-only plan was the sum of two squares. The side walls are emphasised by two large central arches that lead into the semi-elliptical chapels and are flanked by two smaller arches that frame two rectangular-plan niches capped by small, elliptical cupolas.

The wooden **choir** by Marcantonio Zucchi dating to 1517 is of particular interest.

PALAZZO DAZZI
già CORRADI-CERVI

The palazzo was commissioned by, and originally named for, the marchese Captain Gian Francesco Corradi-Cervi (1729-98) and built despite problems over the plans between 1794 and 1797 after a design by the architect Domenico Cossetti, a pupil of Petitot.

The multi-windowed façade is set off by a central pediment supported by two columns and two fluted pilaster-strips with Corinthian capitals. Its severe neoclassical style dates it to the cityscape of the last quarter of the 18th century, when there was a break with Petitot's style in favor of stricter neoclassical forms. *Innocence* (1837), a sculpture by Tommaso Bandini of Parma, stands in the courtyard. The palazzo is privately owned and not open to the public.

PALAZZO RANGONI

The palazzo's present-day appearance apparently dates to 1690 and the marriage of Odoardo Farnese to Dorotea Sofia of Neuburg — the occasion for which the old 16th-century building of the Rangoni counts was redesigned. It gave onto the main processional avenue and hat to be readied as part of the grand backdrop to the duke's magnificent festivities.

The transformation of the building, which became a Farnese residence while remaining the property of the Rangonis, was probably the work of Ferdinando Bibiena; the exterior and interior stucco decorations were done by Giovan Battista Barberini and his pupils.

The façade, which has two orders of windows embellished by volute frames, is emphasized by an outstanding portal flanked by two colossal statues on high pedestals and surmounted by a balustraded balcony emblazoned below with the ducal coat of arms. The interior of the palazzo,

built round a quadrangular courtyard, houses the Prefecture and is not open to the public. It has been almost completely redone, with only the entrance hall and the staircase embellished by Barberini's stuccos remaining.

1. Church of S. Vitale. Chapel of Madonna di Costantinopoli (left transept). The rich plastic decoration is by Domenico and Leonardo Reti. 2. Ex-Cloister of S. Quintino at number 25 Via XX Luglio. 3. 44 Repubblica Street. Palazzo Dazzi, formerly Corrado Cervi. 4. Number 39, Repubblica Street. Palazzo Rangoni, it's the seat of Prefecture, now.

SAN ANTONIO ABATE

The church was founded in 1402 by the monks of St Anthony, Abbot. Cardinal A. Francesco Sanvitale, its preceptor at the beginning of the 18th century, decided to rebuild it, assigning the project to Ferdinando Bibiena, the architect and creator of spectacular stage-designs for the masques put on by the court. Construction was begun in 1712 but was interrupted in 1714 because of the Cardinal Sanvitale's death. In 1759, almost half a century later, work resumed under the direction of Gaetano Ghidetti. Nonetheless, the project remained essentially faithful to Bibiena's conception, despite some changes in the decorative elements.

The church is in Strada Repubblica (the old San Michele), the scene of the grand parades that were held when important personages arrived in Parma. Its location probably gave Bibiena the idea for centring the façade in a grandiose triumphal arch recalling those ephemeral festivities. But it is the interior that fully manifests Bibiena's bent for stage-design, with the double open-grid vault that succeeds perfectly in astonishing the viewer by creating the illusion of a space open to the sky.

The design is a fitting example of Baroque architecture's penchant for the illusionistic, which found its maximum expression in the creation of ceilings that increasingly approximated the vault of heaven.

With an aisle-less nave, apse choir and four side chapels, the Guarini-inspired plan originates from the ideal spatial conjunction of two diagonally-rounded squares forming wedge-shaped spurs that spring from the large arches crossed by the **double groin vault**.

The frescos of the upper vault, which appear through the grid openings, depict St Anthony the Abbot in glory with angels (1766) and are the work of Giuseppe Peroni, who also did the Apparition of Christ to St Anthony on the high altar and the Crucifixion in the first chapel on the left. Peroni, whose works are permeated by a somewhat sentimental piety, had a major influence on art in Parma before neoclassicism.

In the second chapel on the left one finds a Sermon of St John the Baptist painted by Pompeo Batoni in 1777. Of note in the second chapel on the right is G.B. Cignaroli's 1766 altarpiece portraying the Flight into Egypt. The exotic detail of the sphinx is considered a noteworthy stylistic refinement.

The statues of the Beatitudes embellishing the niches are the work of Gaetano Callani of Parma, a painter and sculptor who was a pupil of Peroni's. In this sculpture (*ca.* 1765) he reveals a style inspired by classical models — a neoclassicism almost ahead of its times — which stemmed from his having seen the Roman statues from the Veleia excavations exhibited at Parma in 1761.

1. Church of S. Antonio Abate. View of the double open-work vault with the upper frescos representing S. Antonio Abate on Glory, by G. Peroni. 2. View of the interior with the statues of Beatitudini of G. Gallani. 3. Number 57, Repubblica Street, Palazzo Marchi. 4. Ex-Cloister of S. Sepolcro (Borgo Valorio).

PALAZZO MARCHI

This is one of Parma's most important palazzi. Built 1770-74 by order of the marchese Scipione Grillo after a design by the abbot Furlani, its imposing mass faces Via Repubblica, the once prestigious setting of grandiose parades.

The three-storey structure's façade features a majestic entrance with Doric columns supporting the balcony, facing panels of simulated rustication and a culminating dentil cornice. It is further accentuated by stucco string courses, and its windows, except for those on the top floor, are emphasized by pilaster-strips that alternately support curved and triangular tympana.

From the entry portal one has a view of the two interior courtyards — the first with a Doric colonnade and the second with a garden, originally embellished by an illusionistic background painted on the rear wall. The stone staircase, which divides in scissors fashion after the first flight, is adorned with stucco statues. The interior, with its ornately appointed rooms decorated in stucco, is not open to the public.

SAN SEPOLCRO

Founded *ca.* 1100, the Church of the Holy Sepulchre was completely rebuilt in 1257. The present-day Renaissance façade (1506) was executed by Bartolomeo Pradesoli after a design by Iacopo da Modena. The Mannerist sculptor and architect Simone Moschino probably designed the bell tower (1616). In 1780 the south side of the church on Via Repubblica was redone in the neoclassical style by the architect Antonio Brianti.

The interior, an aisle-less nave with five chapels on each side and two others flanking the presbytery that is framed in turn by gothic arches, has a superb coffered wooden ceiling (1613-17) carved by Lorenzo Zaniboni and Giacomo Trioli.

Noteworthy are the second chapel on the right, with its 1621 painting of the Virgin and Child with Sts Francis of Assisi, Peter, Paul and Augustine by Pier Antonio Bernabei, and the fourth, with a 1754 painting of the Guardian Angel by Cignaroli.

The umbrella vault of the presbytery and the lunettes were frescoed by Cesare Baglione in the late 17th - early 18th century, although the New Testament scenes are all but indistinguishable today. The quadratura or illusionistic architectural background in the apse is attributed to Ferdinando Bibiena (early 18th century). The high altarpiece with the Resurrection (1670) is by Francesco Monti («il Brescianino»).

In the fourth chapel on the left, Sebastiano Galeotti's painting of St Wibald healing an invalid (1723) is marked by deftly drawn yet restless lines in contrasting colours.

On the right wall of the second chapel one finds the painting of St Catherine's Mystical Wedding, by Lion-

ello Spada (1576-1622), who died before completing it.

In the first chapel, frescoed by Cesare Baglione with grotesques and religious scenes that can be ascribed to the late 16th or early 17th century, there is a copy dating to the end of the 17th century and attributed to Alessandro Mari of Correggio's Madonna della Scodella (1530), originally located in the church and which, after an eventful history, entered the National Gallery.

Also noteworthy are, in the antesacristy, the Samaritan woman at the well by Giuseppe Peroni (ca. 1757-1765) and in the sacristy itself, the locally crafted wood furnishings (17th and 18th centuries) and the altarpiece of the Madonna, Jesus, St. John and angels by Girolamo Mazzola Bedoli (mid-16th century).

CONVITTO NAZIONALE MARIA LUIGIA

In 1831 the Duchess Marie Louise merged two existing colleges, the Lalatta (1755) and the College of Nobles (1602) to create the present one bearing her name. It is housed in a famous palazzo built on the site of an ancient Roman amphitheatre of which three salvaged columns and a panel were incorporated and can be seen today on the north side. Here, too, was built Federico Barbarossa's 12th-century imperial palace, known as «the Arena», which later served as the residence of various podestas or ruling nobles. In time it underwent radical alterations, and was acquired in the 16th century by the Lalatta nobles.

Dating to this era are the frescos that decorate the Sala dei Giganti (Giants' Room) and the library's vault, the work of Lattanzio Gambara (1572-73) of Brescia and several local artists, respectively. During the 17th century, the palazzo was the residence of the cardinals Odoardo and Francesco Maria Farnese, taking on the name of Casino degli eremitani (Hermits' House).

After becoming the Marie Louise College, it was further altered between 1836 and 1847 by the ducal architect Nicola Bettoli, who, among others, created the neoclassical façade. The college, which was formally named Convitto Nazionale Maria Luigia in 1896, has an interesting collection of 139 portraits of the most distinguished pupils of the pre-existing College of Nobles, i.e those belonging to the Accademia degli Scelt (Academy of the Elect) founded in 1662 by Ranuccio II Farnese.

1. Via Padre Onorio. Maria Luigia National Boarding School The neoclassic front is by N. Bettoli.

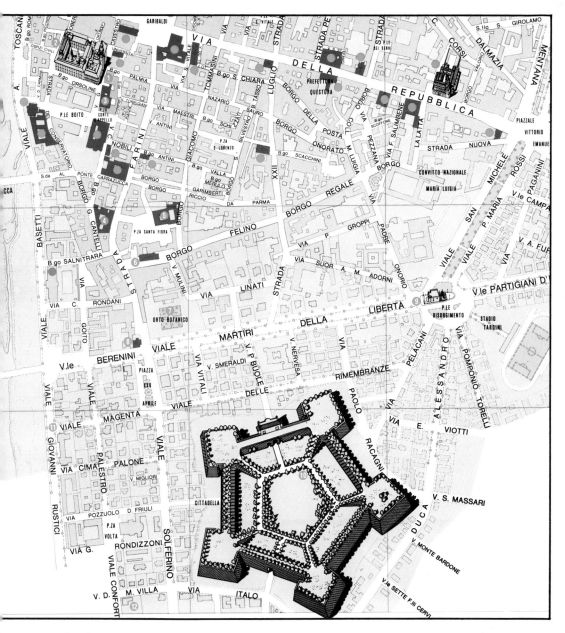

TOUR NO. 6

SAN ROCCO

The church was erected in 1528 to honour a vow made by the citizenry, who had asked St Rocco's protection during an outbreak of the plague.

The original building, with its Greek-cross plan, remained unfinished because of financial difficulties and was completed only in 1598 by the Jesuits, to whom it had been given in 1564 when they were summoned to Parma. However, because the church was small and its central-plan layout was ill-suited to the Jesuits' needs, it was decided almost immediately to build in its stead another more befitting the dignity of the Order.

Rebuilding began in 1737 and the present

church was completed in 1754 under the Bolognese architect Alfonso Torreggiani, who was assisted by his son Antonio. The construction was directed by Adalberto Della Nave of Parma, who altered some of the façade's details while keeping the essential design intact.

The front of the church, crowded by the facing building, is crowned by a curved pediment with two orders, the lower Ionic and the upper composite.

The square-section bell tower (1747) against the east side is by Antonio Bettoli.

The exterior gives absolutely no hint of the interior's illusionistic spatial arrangement — a hall running the entire length with chapels, emphasized by irregular hexagonal forms at the façade end and octagonal ones flanking the presbytery over which the drumless cupola rests.

The single space is accented by very pronounced, almost free-standing columns that gradually recede in perspective towards the presbytery — a scenographic effect in the Bolognese tradition of Vigarani and Bibiena. The walls, with their large windows, were designed by Torreggiani as if they were non-bearing elements, with the result that the chapels go almost unnoticed.

The small tribunes or galleries in carved, lacquered and gilded wood were modelled on those designed by Father Pozzo for the Jesuit church at Trento. In addition to serving the purpose of separating the Jesuits from the congregation during religious services, they also contribute to the interior's lightness and elegance by virtue of their unique rendering.

The stucco decoration of the composite capitals and the ornate woodwork of the tribunes — both bearing the unifying imprint of the Rococo — point to Torreggiani himself, whose projects tended towards a uniformity of ornament and structure, as designer. He is also credited with designing the pulpit and the sedan chair, both of which were carved, gilded and lacquered by local carpenters and craftsmen (1754).

The church's art collection consists mainly of 19th-century works by Parma's academy artists.

Of considerable interest in the small octagonal chapel to the left of the sanctuary is the funerary monument to Giacinta Sanvitale Conti, Duchess of Poli, whose husband, Apio, had it erected upon her death in 1652. The baroque chapel of multi-coloured marble, which shows up rather rigid and cold in the bust of the deceased by an anonymous sculptor, is attributed to Alberto Oliva (17th century), as are the two bronze candelabra angels.

The painting of the Circumcision to the right of the altar is attributed to Giacinto Brandi (1623-1691) of Rome, pupil of Lanfranco.

The sacristy was also designed by Alfonso Torreggiani, as were the decorations and the typically rococo furnishings.

Annexed to the church and now part of the university is the Jesuits' College, which was built during the 17th century, and is a massive rectangle enclosing a courtyard. The severe **Palazzo delle Orsoline** (Ursuline Convent) was built opposite the south side during the same period.

1. Church of S. Rocco. Interior view with wooden tribune with a grate. 2. Palazzo delle Orsoline, dating from XVII century. (B.go delle Orsoline). 3. Aerial view of Collegio dei Gesuiti, now it's the seat of University. 4. «Arrigo Boito» Conservatoire.

1

MUSEO DI STORIA NATURALE DELL'UNIVERSITÀ

Although its original collection dates to 1764, the Natural History Museum was officially established in 1980, following its expansion over the years by such illustrious naturalists as Strobel, Andres and others.

The museum is basically zoological, with its displays of vertebrates being the main attraction, although it has also collections of molluscs and insects. Among its most interesting specimens are the okapi (the museum has a splendid pair of this forest giraffe), the aardvark or African anteater and several other rare species that are found in only a few other monuments.

The museum also houses the African collections of Bottego and Piola, with the latter containing some ethnographic material. The first four volumes of what will be the museum's complete catalogue are currently available.

Annexed to the museum is the «Laboratorio» housing in the main invertebrate collections for teaching and study purposes that can be viewed upon request.

Hours: For schools, Monday-Thursday mornings (9-12) by appointment only (Tel: 208855). For the General Public: Tuesday, Wednesday, Thursday and Saturday, 3-5 p.m. Closed all of August.

PINACOTECA STUARD

The picture gallery or museum, located on premises owned by the Congregation of St Philip Neri boasts a collection of more than two hundred valuable works of art bequeathed in 1834 by Giuseppe Stuard (1791-1834), a man of con-

117

siderable learning and the last descendant of the Tuerdi or Stuerdi family of the Piedmont nobility.

The main body of the collection's paintings are of the Tuscan school of the 14th-15th centuries and features artists such as Bernardo Daddi, Bicci di Lorenzo, Paolo di Giovanni Fei, Nicolò di Tommaso, and Pietro di Giovanni Ambrosi. Other works on exhibit include those by Bartolomeo Schedoni, Giovanni Lanfranco, Guercino, Sebastiano Ricci, Giuseppe Baldrighi, Clemente Ruta, Pietro M. Ferrari, Alberto Pasini, and De Stroebel, still lifes by Felice Boselli, and landscapes and battle scenes by Ilario Spolverini.

Hours: Weekdays 8.30am-12.30pm. Closed Saturdays & Sundays.

1. Stuard Picture-Gallery. Pietro di Giovanni Ambrosi. Christ is entering Jerusalem. (first half of XV century). 2. Bicci di Lorenzo. Polyptych with St. John and St. Thomas (the first half of the XV century). 3. Bicci di Lorenzo. Polyptych with St. James and St. Nicholas (the first half of the XV century). 4. Sebastiano Ricci. S. Francesco di Paola raises a young boy from the dead. 5. The arcade of Via Farini. 6. Via Farini and Palazzo Carmi. 7. Santa Fiora Square. Palazzo Pallavicino. 8. Palazzo Pallavicino. View of the main staircase with statues and frescos of the vault by S. Galeotti.

PALAZZO CARMI

Designed by the ducal architect Paolo Gazzola between 1825 and 1830, the building has belonged to the Carmi family for about a century. Gazzola actually redesigned a 16th-century palazzo on commission from the new owner, Amedeo Rosazza-Pistolet, a Piedmontese entrepreneur who built Parma's major public works during the era of Marie Louise.

With its neoclassical façade and interior, Palazzo Carmi is an example of the change to this new style that some of the buildings on the main streets underwent in the early 19th century.

The façade, with its two short receding wings that fit in with the street's curved perspective, is emphasized in the center, where the piano nobile or main floor is balconied and fluted pilaster-strips with Ionic capitals break up the fenestration and support the tympanum. The interior of the palazzo, built round a courtyard plan but privately owned and not open to the public, is noteworthy for its Salone degli Specchi (Hall of Mirrors), music room, and an octagonal room decorated in Pompeian style with a painted ceiling by Giovan Battista Borghesi. The back of the building in Via Cantelli still preserves its 16th-century appearance.

PALAZZO PALLAVICINO

Built between the end of the 15th century and the beginning of the 16th by the Sforza di Santa Fiora family, it was sold in 1646 to the Pallavicino family, who altered it to its present appearance.

The imposing four-storey façade is characterized by a stately entrance with strong corbels supporting a central balcony and moved by the variety in the orders of windows differing in size and frame. The entrance leads to the elegant courtyard and its grand staircase, adorned with niches, statues and a vault frescoed by Galeotti. On the piano nobile one finds numerous rooms with rich 16th- and 17th-century decorations.

7

8

SANT'ULDARICO

Founded before the year 1000 on the ruins of an ancient Roman theatre, it was the site of a Benedictine convent that was abolished in the Napoleonic era.

The church and the convent were rebuilt in the 15th and early 16th centuries under the patronage of the abbesses of the Carissimi family. Remaining from this period are the impressive Renaissance cloister featuring a brickwork cornice and gallery that has the peculiarity of pointed arches on the short sides and round arches on the long sides. The different-style capitals have decorations that alternate mainly plant motifs with the Carissimi coat of arms bearing a bull.

The church underwent further rebuilding in 1762. Of particular note inside are G.G. Baruffi's carved and inlaid wooden **choir**, commissioned in 1505 by Abbess Cabrina Carissimi, and the two paintings on the side walls of the apse, Esther before Ahasuerus and Judith with the Head of Holofernes dating to 1718. The first known works of Clemente Ruta, they manifest the influence of the Bolognese academy school.

SANTA MARIA DEGLI ANGELI (DELLE CAPPUCCINE)

Originally set against the old city's fortified walls, the church of St Mary of the Angels (also known as St Mary of the Capuchin Nuns) was built in 1569 or 1572 and designed by the architect G.F. Testa to encompass a much venerated Madonna and Child painted on the wall at the time (the devotional image was removed to the Duomo in 1686). The building's site strongly influenced its shape, which is highly contracted longitudinally.

1

2

The church's exterior boasts a triumphal-arch por-
ico with a small **cupola**. The interior is transversely divided into a small nave and aisles emphasized by
arches sprung on coupled Levanto red-marble columns with bases and capitals in Carrara marble. The
octagonal presbytery and its cupola were presumably
built a few years after the church, following the partial
demolition of the defensive fortifications that limited
its space. This explains the different styles of the capi-
als and the staggering of the cornices.

The vast cycle of recently restored pictorial decorations completely covering the interior began in 1588
with the cupola frescos by Gian Battista Tinti. In the
enter, bathed in a golden light, one can see the dove of

. Church of S. Uldarico. The Renaissance cloister. 2. Orto
Botanico. 3. Church of S. Maria degli Angeli, called delle
Cappuccine. The interior. 4. G.B. Tinti, the dome with the rep-
resentation of the Paradise. 5. Detail of the dome.

the Holy Spirit surrounded by cherubs arranged in concentric circles. In the lower bay the main figures of this Heaven stand out amid angels and saintly musicians: the Eternal Godhead facing the altar and the Virgin facing the faithful. The pendentives depict Jesse, Gideon, Moses and Ezekial.

It clearly resembles the magnificent cupola by Correggio in the Duomo, although here the celestial vision is smaller in scale, more intimate and subdued. An exponent of the late 16th century's less hectic artistic milieu, Tinti and his work were strongly influenced by the great painting of the earlier period, especially that of Parma. In the cupola the artist uses a vivid array of Mannerist colours — yellows, violets, greens — that pointedly recall Correggio as well as Anselmi, Parmigianino and Pordenone di Cortemaggiore.

The pictorial decoration of the small nave and aisles dates to 1620. The left aisle is dedicated to the Virgin, the nave in the centre to the Virgin and Christ, and the right aisle to the life of Christ. Executed in mixed media, the scenes in oil on the wall are enclosed in octagonal and oval frames with an intricate fresco decoration of ornamental motifs, angels, sybils and prophets. This is the work of Pier Antonio Bernabei, best known for his decoration of the cupola of S. Maria del Quartiere, and who should probably be credited with the right aisle, and Giovanni Maria Conti, known as «della Camera», who also executed the fine frescos of S. Croce and the Oratorio di S. Ilario. Here too, as in Tinti, Parma's local artistic influences of the 16th century are strong in both. The illusionistic perspective of the late 17th-early 18th century Bibbiena school on the walls expands the nave and aisles laterally, as in a stage set.

The high altarpiece, a *Pietà* by Sebastiano Ricci (1659-1734), is also worthy of mention.

CASINO PETITOT

This small building, inaugurated in 1766 and designed together with the large tree-lined avenue, lo Stradone, that encloses it on the east, by the Bourbon court architect E.A. Petitot, can be considered one of Italy's first *cafés*.

It was the minister Du Tillot who decided to transform the embankment at the end of the developed area between the city and its walls into a straight thoroughfare divided by rows of horse chestnuts into three lanes: the centre for carriages and the sides, with marble benches, for pedestrians. Closing this veritable provincial boulevard is the Casino, a sort of «cube», entirely faced in flat rustication and adorned by a large serliana on the façade. The building served as a meeting place and offered a fine panorama from its attic storey.

Du Tillot's project reveals the typically 18th-century taste for the promenade, which at the time meant the appointed afternoon hour when nobles and the middle class would meet. At the same time particular attention was given to beautifying the cityscape, with park areas coming into their own.

In Parma lo Stradone and its Casino against the town walls became part of the scenic stroll along the walls, which were also lined with chestnut trees at the time.

CITTADELLA

Now encroached on by modern real-property development, la cittadella (The Citadel), another of the imposing Farnese buildings, was erected during the last decade of the 16th century at the very edge of the built-up area outside the city walls, becoming an integral part of them with the construction of connecting walls.

The building, begun in 1591, is the legacy of Duke Alessandro, more soldier than prince, general of Philip II and governor of Flanders, and son of Ottavio. He possessed such an intimate knowledge of defence techniques and military architecture that he even wrote a text about them, which leads one to believe he not only commissioned but probably had a role in designing the citadel of Parma.

Although he was in Flanders, Alessandro personally directed its construction, which was entrusted to the court engineers Giovanni Antonio Stirpio and Genesio Bressani, with the constant

Ripresa aerofotogrammaetrica della Compagnia Generale Ripreseaeree - Parma - conc. S.M.A. n. 68 del 20.02.78.

collaboration of the ducal architect Smeraldo Smeraldi.

The reasons for building a fortress at the time probably had nothing to do with any real defensive need. Parma had become an ally of Spain and was enjoying a period of political stability. Indeed, the citadel was to be used as a prison rather than a bastion of defence. But the overriding concern, apart from any desire to create an imposing symbol of ducal power (if not truly to intimidate his subjects), was the duke's interest in military architecture: he envisaged the building as a challenge, a test of his own competence. There may have been an economic reason that should not be overlooked: in a period of severe famine the construction of a fortress financed entirely by the ruling family would provide work for a great many men.

The citadel, finished by Alessandro's son, Ranuccio, has the conventional pentagonal shape, with bastions at the corners. It was clearly inspired by the fortress at Anvers, whose defensive efficacy Alessandro himself was able to verify during the siege of 1585.

1. The Pentagonal Cittadella. Aerial View. 2. The Cittadella. The XVII century portal by S. Moschino. 3. View of the park of Cittadella.

The citadel, now a public park including a hostel, preserves almost intact its star-plan wall, which still features its greenery and walkways; however, all the other original features — lodgings, stables, watch-towers at the bastions, etc. — have long since disappeared.

The main portal (facing the city), with the exception of the recent brick coping that replaced the primitive four-pitch roof, is original. Designed by the ducal architect Simone Moschino, it reveals early 17th-century decorative taste in its typical bottom rustication and the herms or rectangular pillars terminating in busts supporting the cornice above. The Farnese coat of arms appears in the center.

The rear portal in granite, which opens to the countryside, was also imposing until being destroyed during the last war. In front of it one can see one of the two marble cannons interred during the rebuilding of the entrance and originally located next to the original portal.

VILLA PERNIGOTTI

Mario Stocchi Monti (1880-1950) designed Villa Pernigotti, built in 1911 at the corner of Viale Rustici and Viale Magenta. The building is embellished and heightened by a decoration of large volutes and floral motifs and ranks as one of the most unusual examples of Art Nouveau. It

stands out from the typical buildings of the period, which were the result of a heavy building boom, both public (Moderanno Chiavelli's Post Office) and private (the Bormioli house by Alfredo Provinciali), that was influenced by Art Nouveau, but which in some cases was still tied to a more traditional eclecticism.

MUSEO CINESE

This interesting collection of Chinese art is in the 20th-century palazzo of Foreign Missions. It has actually evolved into two sections, one Chinese and one Ethnological, and was created by Monsignor Guido Maria Conforti, Father Superior of the institute, and later the city's bishop, who wanted to promulgate the cultures of the many countries in which the missions were active as well as to educate young missionaries.

He is to be credited with the idea of collecting artifacts from the various mission countries, to which were added many donated objects, such as those of the sizeable bequest of senatore F. Lampertico in 1900.

At the core is without doubt the Chinese section, a rare and valuable collection. It includes

2

splendid bronzes ranging from the second mill-ennium B.C. to the beginning of our century, cer-amics of considerable value, among which two precious vases of the Pan Shan dynasty dating to the third millennium B.C., watercolours on pa-per and silk, jades, elaborately carved ivories and other works of the decorative arts.

. Rustici Avenue. Villa Pernigotti, one of the most extraordi-nary examples of Liberty architecture in the town. 2. Chinese Museum. «Two colours» vase. Half XVI century. Ming Dynas-y. 3. Kuan Yin Simhanada. Bronze. Ming Dynasty (1368-1644).

Hours: Wed-Sun 3-6pm. Closed Mondays & Tues-days.

COLORNO

A few kilometres outside Parma and not far from the Po River is Colorno, which takes its name from being situated at the point where the Lorno stream flows into the Po (Caput Lurni).

Founded by the Romans, it became an important political and cultural centre in the middle of the 15th century under the Sanseverini family, who turned the old fort into a refined court. In 1612, as part of Ranuccio I Farnese's autocratic governing policy, Colorno was forcefully appropriated by the duke. The vast wooded area surrounding la Reggia (the Royal Palace) made it such a popular venue for noble diversions, spectacular shooting parties in particular, that it fast became the favourite summer retreat first of the Farneses, then the Bourbons and, lastly, Marie Louise.

The present appearance of this splendid villa came about gradually: the quadrilateral plan with the inner courtyard and corner towers dates to the time of Ranuccio II (1646-1694), whereas it was the last of the Farneses, Francesco, who gave it the aspect of a sumptuous residence that it still retains by virtue of the renovations from *ca.* 1712 to 1727 traditionally attributed to Ferdinando Bibiena of Bologna. He redesigned the façade and two sides facing the square to the south, the tower to the west, and the garden to the east, respectively, and subdued the original severity with stately decorations and such scenic elements as the main entrance. With its theatre set up in one of the inner courtyards, its splendid park full of spectacular fountains and magnificent arabesques of a wide variety of tree species, the villa became a miniature Versailles.

Additional modifications were made at the time of Don Filippo of Bourbon around the middle of the 18th century by the ducal architect E.A. Petitot, who redesigned Bibiena's garden stairway as it now appears and the interiors. He also designed part of the furnishings, as the palace was stripped bare when Don Carlo left. Marie Louise is responsible for relandscaping the park in the picturesque English style that still characterizes it in the main today.

Not far from the villa one finds some annex buildings that form part of the royal complex: the

---

1. View of the hills of Torrechiara. 2. Colorno. Aerial view with the ducal group of buildings.

Aranciaia (Orangery) attributed to Bibiena, where citrus trees were kept during the winter and which now houses the local Ethnographic Museum; the **Veneria**, or Hunting Lodge of Don Filippo and now the offices of the Public Welfare Services; and, finally, the **Cappella reale** (Royal Chapel) **of St Liborio** behind the palace designed by Petitot (1791). The latter in particular merits a visit as its state of preservation, including furnishings, especially the organ by the Serassi brothers (1792-1796), makes it a significant example of 17th-century art and religious sentiment. Of note on the outskirts of Colorno are the 17th-century oratories of **Vedole** and **Copermio** and the grandiose **Certosa di Valleserena** (Valleserena Charterhouse), or **Paradigna**, founded by the Cistercians and taken as a model by Stendhal for his famous Charterhouse of Parma.

SAN SECONDO

Fief and official residence of the Rossi family, this castle was built around the mid-15th century by Pier Maria Rossi and renovated by his successors, Troilus I and II, who gave it the appearance of a stately palazzo. Today it is the Town Hall.

Dating to the time of Pietro Maria II (second quarter of the 16th century) are the decorations of what was probably the wedding room, called the Asino d'Oro (Golden Ass), which bears the coat of arms of the Rossis and the Gonzagas in honour of the marriage of Pietro Maria and Camilla (1523). The vault's frescos were inspired by Apuleius' tale of the same title which he translated from a Greek source into Latin and which Matteo Maria Boiardo then translated into Italian. The story, divided into panels that run left to right, is the work of a pupil of Raffaello's who worked on the Vatican loggias.

Another room of considerable interest is the Fasti rossiani (Pageant of the Rossi Family) with 13 large frescos dedicated to the glorious events in the family's history (mid-16th century, era of Troilus II) and attributed to second-generation Mannerist painters of Parma. The attribution is the subject of controversy and has included Bertoja, Mirola, and Mazzoni. The grotesques and landscapes, which strongly resemble those painted in the castles at Torrechiara, Soragna and Sala Baganza at about the same time, are attributed to Cesare Baglione.

Other rooms have frescos dating to the same period nd inspired by Aesop's fables and mythological tales.

BUSSETO

Motoring along the roads of the Po River's owlands, winding through the flat and uniform rms of a countryside not without a certain harm to its monotony, one comes to Busseto, he birthplace and favourite residence of Giuseppe Verdi.

The town's core still preserves nearly unhanged its rectangular shape, once enclosed by alls and square towers in part still extant. Here he remnants of a bygone importance are re-vealed in certain architectonic features and in the stately ornamentation that still characterizes the buildings of the old centre.

Busseto was once the seat of the vast Pallavicino State and reached its political and cultural apex under Odoardo during the first half of the 15th century.

Facing the Piazza named after Verdi are the **Rocca Pallavicino** or fort, completely rebuilt in the 19th century and now the town hall, the Teatro Verdi (1867), the old **Palazzo del Comune** (Town Hall) with its lovely 15th-century terra-cottas, and the 15th-century **Collegiata di San Bartolomeo** (Collegiate Chapter of St Bartholomew).

Also of note just outside the centre is the splendid and imposing 16th-century Villa Pallavicino, now the location of the Museo Civico (Municipal Museum) and, a few kilometres outside of the town in the frazione (village) of **Roncole**, one finds the house where Verdi was born.

Colorno. Palazzo Ducale. To the garden. 2. Paradigna. The istercian Abbey identified in the «Chartreuse» by Stendhal. S. Secondo. La Rocca. 4. Busseto. View of G. Verdi Square th Rocca Pallavicino.

1. Giovanni Boldini. Portrait of the Maestro (oil-painting). The painting is in Milan at the Casa di Riposo G. Verdi. 2. Villa Sant'Agata. The red parlour. 3. The small study with the spinet.

3

Here too the interesting manor, Le Piacentine, where most of director Bernardo Bertolucci's *1900* was filmed on location. Finally, of particular note in the town of S. Agata is the 19th-century villa that was Verdi's summer residence, and which still preserves its original furnishings and many of the composer's possessions. The large park that surrounds it was designed and cared for by the composer himself.

As a tribute to its illustrious citizen, Busseto organizes many vocal and instrumental concerts as well as the prestigious international competition «Voci Verdiane». The town is also the site of a colourful Lenten carnival.

SORAGNA

This 15-century **castle**, which has long been in the Meli Lupi family, was completely transformed into a stately residence in the 17th century.

Noteworthy inside is the room with the late 16th-century frescos depicting Storie di Ercole (Events in the Life of Hercules), attributed to Giulio Campi, and the frieze with fantastic animals, which was influenced by the work of Nicolò dell'Abate. The grotesques in other rooms resemble those at Torrechiara and San Secondo and are attributed to Cesare Baglione.

The residence is adorned with excellent frescos and valuable furnishings and paintings, including still-lifes by F. Boselli. The so-called Galleria dei poeti (Poets' Gallery) dates to 1770 and features busts of ancient and modern poets interspersed with landscapes and mythological scenes by Giovanni Motta of Cremona. A Christ in an aedicule sculpted by G. Amadeo in 1470 is preserved in the chapel.

FONTANELLATO

The 15th-century castle rises above the center of the old town whose name, Fontanelata, derives from the exceptional number of natural springs. Its present appearance is due to the work of the 16th-century architect Smeraldo Smeraldi of Parma. Quadrangular in shape with two rear towers and an entrance in the curtain wall leading to a porticoed courtyard, the castle is enclosed by a crenellated wall and surrounded by a moat. In the early 16th century it became the pro-

. Busseto. Monument of Verdi in the homonymous square. 2. Roncole di Busseto. Native house of G. Verdi. 3. S. Agata. Villa of G. Verdi. 4. Roncole. Parish Church outside. 5. Soragna. The fortress. 6. The poet's arcade.

known as the boudoir of Paola Gonzaga, wife of Galeazzo Sanvitale. The scenes depict the story of Diana and Actaeon from Ovid's Metamorphoses. Having dared to spy on the goddess and her handmaid bathing, Actaeon endured the terrible fate of being changed into a stag and killed by his own dogs. The influence of Correggio's Camera di S. Paolo or St Paul's Room is obvious in the wicker plaitwork that serves as a background to the scenes.

perty of the Sanvitale family, who retained ownership until 1948 when it was bought with all its furnishings by the town.

The castle rooms where the Sanvitale's furnishings and possessions, including the excellent still-lifes by Felice Boselli (*ca.* 1650-1732), are now the Museo Comunale. On the ground floor is the room frescoed by Parmigianino (1503-1540) and traditionally

1. Fontanellato. View of the Rocca. 2. Some houses in the village. 3. Rocca. The interior, first room. 4. Rocca. «Boudoir» of Paola Gonzaga. Parmigianino. Frescos in the vault. 5. Rocca. «Boudoir» of Paola Gonzaga. Parmigianino. Fresco representing Atteone changed into a deer, that is torn by his own dogs. 6. Rocca. «Boudoir» of Paola Gonzaga. Parmigianino... Detail of the vault.

6

As one enters the town one finds the **Santuario** della Beata Vergine del Rosario (Shrine of Our Lady of the Holy Rosary). The 17th-century building with its eclectic 20th-century façade preserves a wooden statue of Our Lady of Miracles (1615) inside a tabernacle on the high altar. Noteworthy are the many ex-votos or votive offerings covering the church's wall in thanksgiving to the Madonna di Fontanellato, who is invoked especially for accidents.

1

1. Fontanellato. Santuario. Miraculous statue of the Vergine del Rosario (1615). 2. Santuario della Beata Vergine del Rosario. The twentieth-century front is eclectic style. 3. Fidenza. Duomo. The front. 4. The three portals of the front.

FIDENZA

Founded by the Romans on the Via Emilia between Parma and Piacenza, Fidenza was destroyed in the 5th century. During the early Middle Ages the remains of San Donnino, a beheaded Roman martyr, were found on the left bank of the Stirone. Here a small rustic chapel, which appears in records dating to 830 as a parish church, was erected in his honour. The medieval village that took its name from the martyred saint arose round it and grew along with his veneration.

The village of San Donnino became the main centre of the area's pilgrimage because of its strategic position at the point where the Via Emilia crosses the strada Francigena or strada Romea, which led from France and Lotharingia (Lorraine) through the Mt. Bardone Pass to Rome. This explains how in so small a town as this a cathedral of such importance came to be built, even benefiting from the art of Benedetto Antelami and his craftsmen.

Between the end of the 11th and the beginning of the 12th centuries the first large basilica began to rise on the site of the rude chapel. It underwent many changes at the beginning of the 13th century at the hands of Antelami before building was interrupted because of the untimely demise of Oberto Pallavicino, lord of the village and patron of the church.

3

The rough unfinished façade is flanked by two towers and features three portals with a two-column portico or *prothyrum*. The architrave of the main portal depicts scenes of the martyrdom of San Donnino, who was a cubicular or bed-chamber attendant of the emperor Maximian (3rd century A.D.), followed by those of his miracles. Apostles and prophets are depicted on the archivolt or underarch.

Two tablets on the left tower depict Herod ordering the Slaughter of the Innocents and the Journey of the Magi.

An unidentified figure of noble lineage is sculpted on the portico's lefthand acroterion; the tympanum has a tripartite scene with Charlemagne (left), Pope Adrian II placing the mitre on the head of the Archpriest of Borgo San Donnino (centre) and a pilgrim about to enter church (right). This is a portrayal of the papal and imperial privileges granted to the town, which always remained faithful to the emperor. A continuous zoophorus or frieze with animal reliefs framed by lozenges graces the archivolt, which is supported by telamones or atlantes from an earlier period. In the lunette is an enthroned Madonna and Child with pious women.

The capital of the demi-pillars depicting Daniel in the lion's den supports a statue of Simon the Apostle indicating the road to Rome. Beside the saint is a tablet with the Adoration of the Magi and St Joseph's Dream underlined by a singularly beautiful floral-patterned frieze beneath which the story of San Donnino begins.

On the side of the central portal in two niches are statues of David and Ezekiel framed by an unusual representation of families of rich and poor pilgrims being invited to enter the church by an angel. Above the last episode in the saint's story is a tablet with Elijah being carried off to heaven in a chariot of fire.

The acroterion of the small portal on the right depicts St Raymond, a poor wayfarer probably meant to symbolise the virtues of poverty. In the tympanum there is a sainted bishop, in the archivolt a zoophorus framed by plant-loop motifs of Byzantine inspiration, and in the lunette St Michael and the dragon.

On the right tower there is a heavily worn relief of the face of Alexander the Great above which is a continuous fascia with allegorical figures representing in turn the struggle between Good and Evil as an encounter between wild animals, Discord as two figures pulling each other's ears, and Seduction or Temptation as blatant courtship; these are followed by a procession of wayfarers on the south side. The decorative

reliefs continue on the apse with a representation of the months.

The bell tower dates to 1569.

The interior, with its women's galleries stripped bare because of an improper 20th-century restoration, is divided into nave and flanking aisles by series of compound piers of alternating light and heavy clusters supporting the groin vaults. The original spatial appearance was altered in the 15th and 16th centuries when the chapels in the aisles were opened.

In the curvature of the apse wall are traces of a 13th-century fresco of the Last Judgement, while the vault features 15th-century sculptures.

The church, which has no transept, ends in a deep choir under which is a large three-aisle crypt holding the sarcophagus of San Donnino. The enthroned Madonna and Child attributed to Benedetto Antelami is noteworthy. Of the sculptures, the statues of David and Ezekiel, the two families of pilgrims and the two column-bearing lions of the major prothyrum are attributed to Antelami because of the quality of the execution; the other pieces have been attributed to his school.

Stylistically, the cathedral is a reworking and synthesis of Lombard and Provençal Romanesque.

Under Fascism, the town reverted to its original Roman name, Fidenza, which it has since retained.

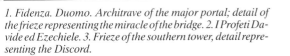

1. Fidenza. Duomo. Architrave of the major portal; detail of the frieze representing the miracle of the bridge. 2. I Profeti Davide ed Ezechiele. 3. Frieze of the southern tower, detail representing the Discord.

Artesian well.

Panoramic view and covered swimming pool.

SALSOMAGGIORE

Salsomaggiore, the third-largest town in the province of Parma, takes its name and derives its revenue from the providential abundance of its natural mineral springs, used since Roman times as a source of salt and since the last century, starting with Dr. Lorenzo Berzieri, for their therapeutic properties. It was early in this century that it became an important spa-cum-tourist centre, when Galileo Chini promoted its Art Nouveau look that still typifies it today. He even designed the decorations of such buildings as the **Terme Berzieri** (Berzieri Hot Springs) (1913-1923) designed by Ugo Giusti and the **Grand Hotel** by Luigi Broggi, already up at the turn of the century.

These are the spa's most important buildings and, along with the large tree-lined avenues, the parks and the recent ultra-modern Terme Zoia, its most distinctive features.

Traditionally the site of a great deal of social activity, Salsomaggiore annually hosts the Miss Italy Contest and in recent years the «Salso Film and TV Festival».

ew of Terme Berzieri.

ice outside view of Terme Berzie-
and two partial views of the
eautiful interiors.

Duomo.

Night view of the fountain.

146

Mazzini Park.

The little lake.

SALA BAGANZA

The **castle** built in 1477 by Giberto III Sanvitale was acquired later by the Farnese family, who used it as a summer residence. Its present appearance is the result of 19th-century alterations.

The interior preserves some excellent works of art. The chapel on the first floor (probably commissioned by Barbara Sanseverino) has a vault decorated with climbing roses that serve as background for putti bearing the symbols of the Passion (*ca.* 1569), attributed to Bernardino Campi of Cremona. It was clearly influenced by Correggio's Camera di S. Paolo and the frescos by Parmigianino in the Fontanellato castle. The so-called Sala dell'Apoteosi («Room of the Apotheosis»), built at the behest of Antonio Farnese, was painted by Sebastiano Galeotti in 1727 with allegorical representations of the Arts and Virtues inspired by pagan mythology and Christianity.

1. Baganza Room. View of the Rocca. 2. Rocca. B. Campi, the vault of the chapel. 3. Torrechiara. View of the XV century castle.

2

148

TORRECHIARA

The earliest record of a small fortress is in a 1259 list of castles that the Podesta of Parma ordered to be demolished. Battered by the vagaries of politics and the stormy events of history, the castle, in ruins, was rebuilt (1448-1460) by Pier Maria Rossi. It then fell into the hands of the Sforza family; in 1503 it was bought by the Pallavicinos, thereafter inherited by the Sforza Cesarini family and, in 1912, purchased by the Italian government.

Built on the top of a hill and still surrounded by the old wall-enclosed village, the castle is one of the most important examples of Renaissance courts in the Parma area. The castle's architec-ture is Lombard in style and substantially intact. It has a square plan with four crenellated towers.

Of particular artistic and historic interest inside is the so-called *Camera d'oro* (Gold Room), frescoed in the mid-15th century by Benedetto Bembo. The frescos on the vault and walls are entirely dedicated to Pier Maria Rossi's love for Bianca Pellegrini of Como, portrayed as characters in a courtly romance. Playing on the name Pellegrini (pilgrim), the artist depicts her as a pilgrim with cloak and staff travelling across her lover's vast estates, depicted with extraordinary topographical fidelity. In the lunettes, the two lovers first appear enshrined in aedicules as they are struck by Cupid; then Pier Maria pledges his sword to Bianca,

who, in the next scene crowns him with a laurel wreath. Concluding the sequence of courtly love and chivalry is the portrayal of a knighted Pier Maria and his richly attired lady.

The Camera d'oro takes its name from the terracotta tiles (on the lower part of the walls) bearing the Rossi coat of arms: two entwined hearts, a castle with raised drawbridge and the initials of the two lovers tied with a ribbon bearing the inscription «nunc et semper» (now and forever). Also of note are the frescoed rooms, including the Salone dei Giocolieri (Jugglers' Room) painted by Cesare Baglione (late 16th-early 17th century) depicting acrobatic feats framed by grotesques.

Pier Maria dedicated to Bianca another **castle, Roccabianca**, whose name clearly refers to her. He had this castle frescoed with the story of Griselda from the Decameron in further celebration of their love.

2

1. Torrechiara. Castle. «Golden Room». B. Bembo, the vault.
2. «Golden Room». B. Bembo. Detail with Bianca Pellegrini.
3. «Golden Room». Detail of the tiles of the walls.

3

PARMESAN CHEESE

The Parmesan cheese is still made as it was seven centuries ago, with essential and authentic ingredients: the good milk of this particular area, the fire and the rennet, with the good old methods, with the art and patience of the dairyman. And then it grows old naturally for two years and more; and this is work, too, because you must clean and turn the cheese, you must take care and control it. It means risk and anxiety too, because the miracle of the perfect ripening is essentially entrusted to nature.

It's made leaving from the dairy, where the milk of the growers arrives; this milk has very special quality due to the environmental characteristics and the strict feeding standard of the cattle. This standard wants the prevailing employment of fresh forage or from pasture and forbids some food. This milk is also good for the particular dairy ability of the cows, that are grown with particular care. They use the milk of two milkings: the evening milk rests all the night long, the morning milk rests in basins for about an hour. After a partial skimming of the evening milk, it is poured with the morning milk into a particular copper boiler, having the shape of an upside down bell, they add ferment whey to this milk. It's

a very old practice that makes the acidimeter degree of milk higher and leads the milk to a suitable fermentation.

After the first slow cooking they add the rennet and they wait for the coagulation that take place 12-15 minutes later. After this, the coagulated product is broken and cooked again on a slow fire but at higher temperature than the first. 30 minutes later the curds are taken from the boiler and put into a wooden or metal mould.

The following operations want to obtain its perfect particular shape, salting, sundrying, the first seasoning in the farmhouse and later in par-

1

154

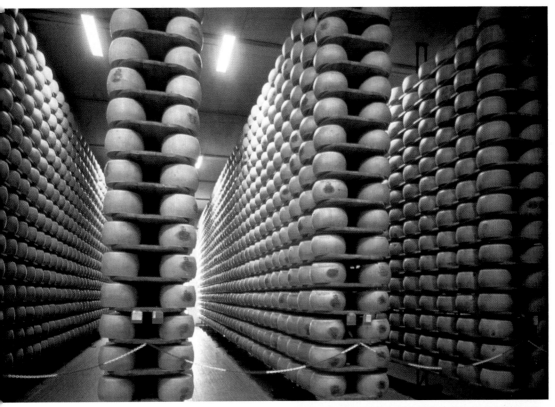

icular warehouses for the final seasoning.

The branding is an important distinguishing element of every cheese that has a specific birth certificate stating the good result of a year's work, the old processing accuracy by the growers and certifies the date of production.

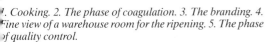

1. Cooking. 2. The phase of coagulation. 3. The branding. 4. Fine view of a warehouse room for the ripening. 5. The phase of quality control.

5

PARMA HAM

Historical Outline

The Roman colonization, dating from 180 B.C., created in Agro Emiliano the environmental premises for the development of great agricultural and zootechnical activities. Particularly in Parma area at the time there spread pig, cattle and ovine breeding. The presence of great quantities of acorns in every part of the area helped an important development of the wild pig breeding, because the acorn was the chosen feeding to fatten this animal. At the time there was the pressing necessity to preserve food, and meat particularly, as long as possible to face the frequent times of famine hanging over the people. For this reason, the problem of meat preserving was widely treated by authors and historians of the ancient times.

We have few and incomplete news about salting and seasoning of Parma ham, in the years, even if we know that at the beginning of 1400 in the province they used meat salting methods that were very similar to the actual ones.

As far as back the XVI century, they described the famous cold cuts of Emilia that distinguished themselves for their particular fragrance; in that period Parma area became famous as the most important centre for the highly quality production and its seasoners, salters and exporters could excel.

1

2

By the spread of better agricultural and zoo-technical conditions, and particularly by the development of dairy activity, also the pig breed-ing had a substantial boost thanks to a new and most rational feeding; at the same time they be-gan a slow but systematic selection of pig breeds.

So they created the conditions for a further im-portant development in the production of hams to be seasoned and quickly they changed the family production into the industrial one. Then they increased the commercial contacts with the nearest areas and little by little, by a widespread expansion, the product was known and appreci-ated not only in the national territory but also abroad.

Processing

The processing of Parma ham can be divided into the following phases: trimming, salting, rest, drying, larding, seasoning. They are practised, nowadays, as they used to be once, following the traditional methods.

1. Salting working. 2. Drying on a balcony. 3. Larding. 4. Branding. 5. Warehouse room for the seasoning.

PARMA

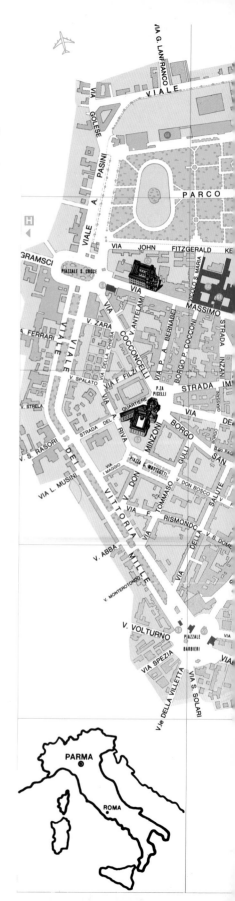

Legenda:

1 - Monumento a Vittorio Bottego
2 - Monumento alla Vittoria
3 - Palazzo della Pilotta (Museo Nazionale d'Antichità, Teatro Farnese, Biblioteca Palatina, Museo Bodoniano, Galleria Nazionale)
4 - Piazza Ghiaia
5 - Monumento al Partigiano
6 - Ara del Monumento a G. Verdi
7 - Camera di S. Paolo (affreschi del Correggio)
8 - Ex Palazzo di Riserva: Museo «Lombardi» - Poste centrali
9 - Chiesa della SS. Trinità o Oratorio dei Rossi
10 - Ex chiesa di S. Barnaba
11 - Ex chiesa e monastero di S. Francesco del Prato
12 - Oratorio della Concezione
13 - Palazzo Borri
14 - Chiesa di S. Benedetto
15 - Cattedrale
16 - Vescovado
17 - Battistero
18 - Chiesa e Convento di S. Giovanni Evangelista
19 - Storica Spezieria di S. Giovanni Evangelista
20 - Palazzo del Comune
21 - Palazzo del Governatore
22 - Chiesa di S. Pietro
23 - Chiesa della Steccata
24 - Chiesa di S. Alessandro
25 - Teatro Regio
26 - Chiesa di S. Lucia
27 - Chiesa di S. Vitale
28 - Chiesa di S. Cristina
29 - Chiesa di S. Quintino
30 - Palazzo Rangoni
31 - Palazzo Dazzi già Corradi Cervi
32 - Chiesa di S. Antonio Abate
33 - Palazzo Miari già Buralli
34 - Palazzo Marchi (Istituto di Studi Verdiani)
35 - Chiesa di S. Sepolcro
36 - Chiesa di S. Michele dell'Arco

37 - Ex chiesa di S. Andrea
38 - Chiesa di S. Rocco
39 - Palazzo dell'Università (Museo Zoologico Eritreo Bottego)
40 - Chiesa del Carmine
41 - Conservatorio di musica «A. Boito»
42 - Palazzo del Tribunale
43 - Pinacoteca Stuard
44 - Chiesa di S. Marcellino
45 - Chiesa di S. Tommaso
46 - Palazzo Soragna-Tarasconi
47 - Palazzo Carmi
48 - Palazzo Pallavicino
49 - Chiesa e Chiostro di S. Uldarico
50 - Oratorio delle Cappuccine
51 - Orto Botanico
52 - Stradone e Casino del Petitot
53 - Cittadella
54 - Museo d'Arte cinese ed etnografico (Palazzo Missioni Estere)
54 bis - Ponte Romano
55 - Oratorio della Madonna delle Grazie
56 - Casa Museo Toscanini
57 - Chiesa della SS. Annunziata
58 - Porta S. Francesco
59 - Barriera Bixio
60 - Ospedale Vecchio (Archivio di Stato)
61 - Oratorio di S. Ilario
62 - Torri di S. Francesco di Paola o dei Paolotti
63 - Chiesa di S. Maria del Quartiere
64 - Chiesa di S. Croce
65 - Palazzo Ducale
66 - Palazzetto del Giardino
67 - Certosa (Via Mantova)
68 - Ente Mostra Internazionale delle Conserve Alimentari
69 - Camera di Commercio I.A.A.
70 - Ferrovie dello Stato
71 - Autostazione
72 - Vigili Urbani (tel. 33132)
73 - A.P.T.
74 - Villa Pernigotti

The Publisher wishes to thank the Direction of the Soprain-tendenza alla Galleria Nazionale of Parma for the active and positive collaboration given in the research and participation of the photographic images present in this guide; the Associazione Italia Nostra of Colecchio, Parma, the Consorzio del Parmigiano Reggiano and the Consorzio del Prosciutto di Parma for the photographic contribution provided.

Photographs by
Foto Zoom di F. Furoncoli - Parma
Fotoscientifica - Parma
Compagnia Generale Ripreseaeree - Parma
Foto Ceresa - Parma
Foto E. Bertinelli - Parma

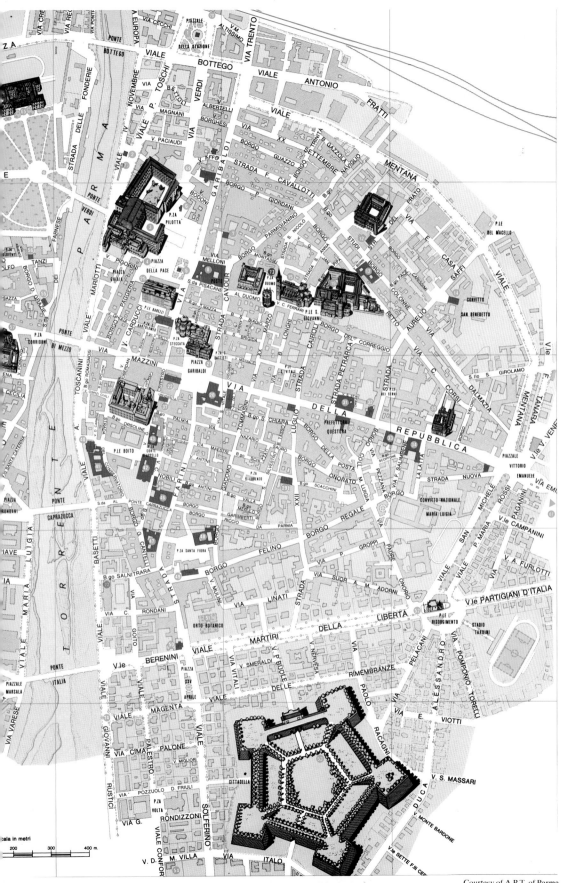

Courtesy of A.P.T. of Parma

PELLEGRINO PARMENSE
ROCCABIANCA
S. SECONDO P.SE
SISSA
SORAGNA
BARDI
VARSI
VARANO MEL.
FONTANELLATO
CASTELGUELFO
NOCETO
PIETRAMOGOLANA
TORRECHIARA
COMPIANO
FELINO
SALA BAGANZA

PARMA

MONTECHIARUGOLO

CREMONA
ZIBELLO
ROCCABIANCA
FIUME PO
BUSSETO
SISSA
SORAGNA
S. SECONDO P.
COLORNO
MILANO
FONTANELLATO
SORBOLO
MANTOVA
FIDENZA
A1 AUTOSTRADA DEL SOLE
BOLOGNA
SALSOMAGGIORE TERME
CASTELGUELFO
NOCETO
TABIANO
PARMA
COLLECCHIO
MONTECHIARUGOLO
PELLEGRINO P
SALA BAGANZA
MONTICELLI TERM
FELINO
A 15
VARANO DEI MELEGARI
FORNOVO
VARSI
BOSCHI DI BARDONE
TORRECHIARA
A 15
LANGHIRANO
BARDI
CALESTANO
ROCCA DI PIETRAMOGOLANA
TIZZANO
BEDONIA
BERCETO
CORNIGLIO
COMPIANO
SCHIA
BORGO VAL DI TARO
PONTREMOLI
MONCHIO
SESTRI LEV.
LAGO SANTO LAGONI
PRATO SPILLA
AULLA

Courtesy of A.P.T. of Parma